Founder and Contributing Editor:
    Lyndon H. LaRouche, Jr.
Editorial Board: *Lyndon H. LaRouche, Jr.,*
    Antony Papert, Gerald Rose, Dennis Small,
    Nancy Spannaus, Jeffrey Steinberg, William
    Wertz
Editor: *Nancy Spannaus*
Managing Editors: *Bonnie James, Susan Welsh*
Technology Editor: *Marsha Freeman*
Book Editor: *Katherine Notley*
Graphics Editor: *Alan Yue*
Photo Editor: *Stuart Lewis*
Circulation Manager: *Stanley Ezrol*

INTELLIGENCE DIRECTORS
Counterintelligence: *Jeffrey Steinberg, Michele*
    Steinberg
Economics: *John Hoefle, Marcia Merry Baker,*
    Paul Gallagher
History: *Anton Chaitkin*
Ibero-America: *Dennis Small*
Russia and Eastern Europe: *Rachel Douglas*
United States: *Debra Freeman*

INTERNATIONAL BUREAUS
Bogotá: *Javier Almario*
Berlin: *Rainer Apel*
Copenhagen: *Tom Gillesberg*
Houston: *Harley Schlanger*
Lima: *Sara Madueño*
Melbourne: *Robert Barwick*
Mexico City: *Gerardo Castilleja Chávez*
New Delhi: *Ramtanu Maitra*
Paris: *Christine Bierre*
Stockholm: *Ulf Sandmark*
United Nations, N.Y.C.: *Leni Rubinstein*
Washington, D.C.: *William Jones*
Wiesbaden: *Göran Haglund*

ON THE WEB
e-mail: eirns@larouchepub.com
www.larouchepub.com
www.executiveintelligencereview.com
www.larouchepub.com/eiw
Webmaster: *John Sigerson*
Assistant Webmaster: *George Hollis*
Editor, Arabic-language edition: *Hussein Askary*

EIR (ISSN 0273-6314) *is published weekly*
(50 issues), by EIR News Service, Inc.,
P.O. Box 17390, Washington, D.C. 20041-0390.
(703) 777-9451

European Headquarters: E.I.R. GmbH, Postfach
Bahnstrasse 9a, D-65205, Wiesbaden, Germany
Tel: 49-611-73650
Homepage: http://www.eirna.com
e-mail: eirna@eirna.com
Director: Georg Neudecker

Montreal, Canada: 514-461-1557

Denmark: EIR - Danmark, Sankt Knuds Vej 11,
basement left, DK-1903 Frederiksberg, Denmark.
Tel.: +45 35 43 60 40, Fax: +45 35 43 87 57. e-mail:
eirdk@hotmail.com.

Mexico City: EIR , Calz de los Gallos 39 interior 2,
Col Plutarco E Calles,
Del. Miguel Hidalgo, CP 11350,
Mexico, DF. Tel 5318-2301, 6306-8363, 6306-8361

Canada Post Publication Sales Agreement
#40683579

Postmaster: Send all address changes to *EIR*, P.O.
Box 17390, Washington, D.C. 20041-0390.

I0437739

From the Editors

Kesha Rogers, shown on our cover campaigning for the runoff election in the Texas Democratic primary race for Senate, is fast emerging as a national spokeswoman for emergency action to reverse the drought that is devastating the western United States. In our *Political Economy* section, we publish presentations from her joint webcast with LaRouche Democrat Michael Steger of San Francisco, who is running in the Democratic primary against Nancy Pelosi. As the two candidates elaborate, Texas and California are not only the largest American states by population, but also the largest agricultural producers—and both have been slammed by the worst drought on record. See *National* for an update on Rogers' campaign.

Joining in the webcast was Ben Deniston of the LaRouche Science Team, who documented that the drought is by no means the result of man-made global warming, but rather of solar cycles that likely signify future global *cooling*—and worsening drought. Rogers, Steger, and Deniston lay out the policy solutions required.

In *Economics*, we feature a fact sheet on "fracking"—which many people believe is a boon because it gives us cheap gas and oil, but which in fact is wrecking the water supply and agriculture.

Internationally, as Jeff Steinberg reports, the Geneva accord among the U.S., Russia, Ukraine's puppet government, and the EU has already broken down, and the danger of war that could spiral out of control remains great. See the statement by 27 Ukrainian political leaders on the threat of civil war. But opposition to the U.S.-EU policy is growing, with even the head of Britain's MI6 declaring that "it's not worth starting World War III over Ukraine."

From Helga Zepp-LaRouche's recent trip to China, we include an interview with her by the Chinese CCTV program "Dialogue," on the potential represented by President Xi Jinping's "New Silk Road."

Lyndon LaRouche contributes two features to this issue, a short discussion of the American System of political economy, originated by Alexander Hamilton; and an in-depth study of "The Incompetence of Twentieth-Century Science Education," The latter is a revised and expanded version of an article we ran in our April 4 issue.

EIR Contents

EIRNS/Sylvia Spaniolo

EIR Political Economy

EMERGENCY CAMPAIGN WEBCAST

Beat the Drought, From Texas to California

The Kesha Rogers for Senate campaign in Texas and the Michael Steger for Congress campaign in California's 12th Congressional District (San Francisco) held a joint webcast on the drought crisis on April 12. Steger, who is running against House Minority Leader Nancy Pelosi for the Democratic nomination, spoke from San Francisco; Rogers and host Harley Schlanger spoke from San Antonio, Texas; and Benjamin Deniston of the LaRouchePAC Science Team spoke from Northern Virginia.

Schlanger introduced the proceedings by saying:

"The purpose of this event is to direct the attention of citizens to the immediate crisis we face, with the drought that is destroying agricultural production, and also the potential for life in the western United States and the Southwest. This is a drought that is now in its fifth year. It's leading to a collapse of production, in agriculture, in livestock. In California, we've seen the state Water District shut off water supplies to the richest agricultural areas in the world. And here in San Antonio, we're near Mead Lake, which as of a month ago was at 3% of its capacity.

"So we're going to be addressing this question of the collapse of the physical economy of the United States, and worldwide, a physical economy which is reflected in the imminent blowout of the global financial system. And that's why there's a war drive from the British Empire, which is part of what we're addressing here: that we have a President in the United States who's functioning as an asset of the British Empire, of the financial interests that ran up the biggest speculative bubble in world history, which popped in 2008. And now they're

building a new bubble! At the same time, they're preparing what's called a 'bail-in,' which means *they're coming for you!* What you think is your money, your savings, your pensions, are going to be gone, are going to be wiped out. By intent. *And they can't put it back together.*

"Now there are solutions, and these are solutions that are uniquely being presented by these two campaigns."

Kesha Rogers, Schlanger reported, came in second in the Democratic primary, and is in the May 27 runoff for the Democratic nomination for the U.S. Senate—"much to the chagrin of the Obama team that was running the campaign of her opponent." Michael Steger is campaigning in San Francisco, as well as in the Imperial Valley and the Central Valley, agricultural areas which are being shut down.

"These two states are important," Schlanger said, "not just because California and Texas are the two largest states in population; but they also represent the most advanced agriculture, and science and technology, in the country. And the solutions to the crisis rest with a change in the financial system, to a Hamiltonian credit system, and, at the same time, with investment in the areas of science and technology that provide solutions.

"So if you're here for that, good. We need activists, people who will take up these ideas. You'll see in the cases of Kesha and Michael, two national and international leaders who aren't afraid to tell you the truth. And ultimately, the truth comes down to: What will *you* do to save this nation and the future?"

The video of the webcast is available at http://www.kesharogers.com.

Ben Deniston

Junk the Insane Green Policy, To Counter the Drought in the West

Kesha Rogers asked me to give brief opening remarks on the reality of the economic crisis and the scientific work we're doing in the Basement Team, specifically related to the economic crisis. I'm going to try to sketch a broad overview, moving quickly....

We're in a major drought crisis. The majority of the state of California is in a state of severe drought (**Figure 1**). California and Texas are leading the nation in the crisis drought conditions, which are also a problem all over the United States. In Texas, there are communities that are literally running out of water.

Fracking is an issue that is accelerating this crisis— this insane policy of using fresh water to pull oil and gas out of the ground—and there are cities where people are turning on the tap and nothing comes out, which has actually happened in a few cases.

In California, the last I heard was half a million acres, 500,000 acres, of the most highly productive farmland are going to go unplanted this year, because of the drought.

In Texas, the cattle herd has collapsed by a fifth, by 20% over the last five years.

So, there are crises in these states, but as has been well understood already by anybody thinking, this has national implications and global implications for the food supply: the food that people need to survive in this country.

We Can't 'Conserve' Our Way Out

So, the point is we need to get serious about this crisis. The entire West is in danger; the entire country is in danger. And what people need to walk away here with is a very clear sense that we need to make a decision as a country, to abandon this green policy, this environmentalist policy of no major water projects, no economic growth, no investment in fission and fusion power—the policy that has dominated the United States for the past 30-40 years. Either we decide to break with that policy and take an active role in improving the land

kesharogers.com

LaRouche Basement team member Ben Deniston addresses the joint Texas-California town hall meeting by video April 12.

of the country, developing the country with NAWAPA [the proposed North American Water and Power Alliance], with thermonuclear fusion power as a critical driver, or we're not going to have a nation.

That is the reality that is facing this country, the state of Texas, the state of California, right now, today. And we have to be serious, and stop deluding ourselves, and address this for what it is.

There is a myth floating around, that if we just buckle down, save up some water for the next year, we can kind of scoot by this drought and come out okay in the next year or the next two years or so. But I want to make very clear that this is a wholly unfounded and dangerous assumption to make. There is no reason to believe that we're going to be going into a period when we're going to have the drought conditions alleviated by any natural means. This is typified by California, where it is already the worst drought on record—and the records go back some 100-150 years. Additional studies have shown this is the worst drought in 500 years, which is based on analyzing tree rings, other proxy evidence, records from the biosphere, from life,

FIGURE 1
U.S. Drought Monitor - Total U.S.
April 8, 2014 (Released Thursday, April 10, 2014) Valid 8 a..m. EDT

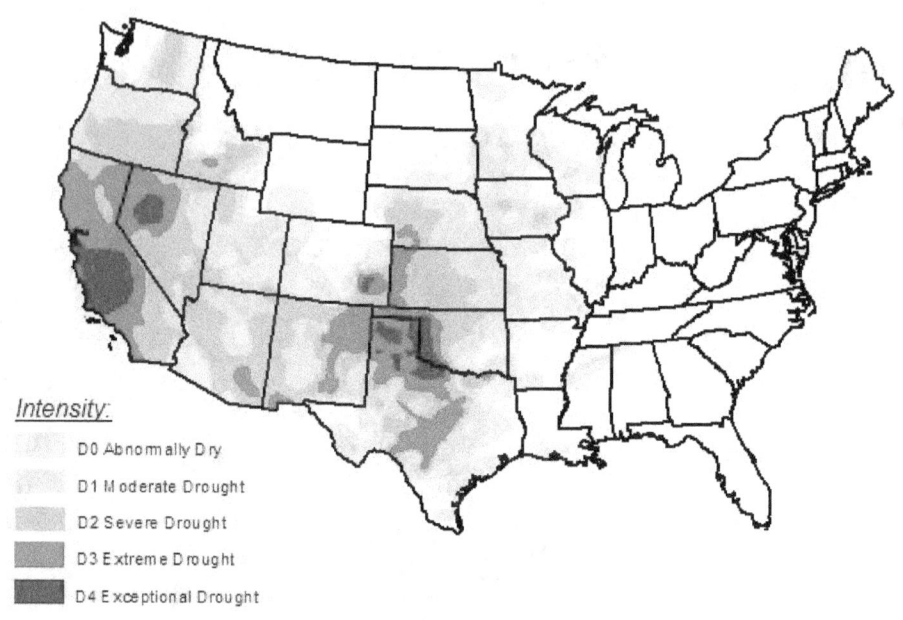

Intensity:

D0 Abnormally Dry

D1 Moderate Drought

D2 Severe Drought

D3 Extreme Drought

D4 Exceptional Drought

DMC-UNL

Drought condidtions ranging from Abnormally Dry to Exceptional Drought blanket California, Texas, and much of the rest of the West.

from the environment, that show the conditions going back further.

Climate and the Sun

But even that doesn't tell the whole story. There was a very important study put out by university researchers in California, indicating that in California and the region of the West, the past century, from say 1900 to 2000, roughly, has been among the wettest centuries in the past 7,000 years. That this 100-year period, the period in which we built our irrigation systems, our dams, our water management projects, was a period that was actually anomalously wet, wetter than it usually it is in the West. So the assumption that we're going to continue to have that level of water availability that we had over the past century, is highly unlikely, given the fact that over the past 7,000 years, seven millennia, this century was one of the wettest. And that's natural climate change—not this bunk that's floating around, trying to blame you for driving your car and destroying the planet, which is totally scientifically absurd—but real climate change, driven

by factors like the Sun, solar activity, and the relationship of solar activity to galactic activity. That relationship between solar activity and galactic activity causes natural fluctuations that life on this planet has to deal with.

So, this is the reality that we're looking at. And we need to take actions that will allow mankind to improve the territory; to use higher forms of energy—nuclear fusion; to use major water projects powered by nuclear fusion, to transform the land area, to transform the territory. And that is the decision we have to make....

I want to take a few minutes to look specifically at the activity of the Sun. We'll take a few steps, on larger and larger time cycles. **Figure 2** is an image of the Sun taken every single year, over the course of one solar cycle: 1996-2006. This is an image taken in X-rays, and you can see that every 10 or 11 years, the Sun goes through a regular cycle, starting off relatively weak, with less activity. It's still warm, you still get sunlight, the Sun doesn't stop shining, but it's less in-

FIGURE 2
X-ray Images of the Sun over One Solar Cycle

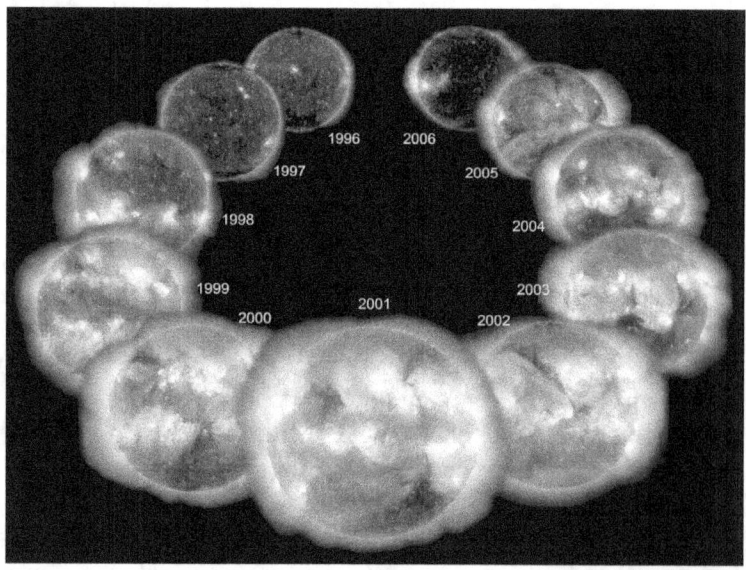

1996   2006
1997   2005
1998   2004
1999   2003
2000   2001   2002

Steele Hill, NASA/ESA

tense, less energetic. It doesn't have as much activity going on. And then over a period of about 5-6 years, on average, it will get more active. It peaked in 2001 and then began to decline again. This is a regular pattern.

Now, what has been a matter of increasing concern among serious scientific thinkers—people who aren't bought off by the "man-made global warming" hoax—is that the Sun is weakening. It's not weakening just in terms of a normal cycle—every 11 years it gets weak again—but *the whole cycle itself is getting less intense.* The peak of the solar cycle is less intense than the previous cycles....

You can see that in **Figure 3**, 400 years of sunspot observations. Sunspots are a very good measure of the overall activity of the Sun, and you can see, over the past 400 years, these roughly 11-year cycles. And you can see clearly that the height of the maximum varies a fair amount. If you go back far enough, say to about 1800, you had a few solar cycles that were very weak. If you go back a little bit farther, to around 1650-1700, you have what's been referred to as the Maunder Minimum, when the Sun, as far as we understand, basically shut down. It continued to put out sunlight, but it was a very quiet phase. It wasn't magnetically active, it wasn't ejecting a lot of material; it was a period, as far as we understand, when there were little or no solar cycles. The Sun basically went to sleep for 50 or 60 years, and we didn't have any solar activity, so far as we can tell. Obviously, the instrumentation was very primitive back then, and this is based mostly on visual observations of sunspots.

The Onset of Global Cooling?

The point is, what was the effect on the Earth? During this Maunder Minimum period, you had a major phase of global cooling. When the Sun became less active, the response on the Earth was a period of major cooling—and not just a little bit cooler here and there, but enough to make a significant impact on society. Places where you could have crops, you couldn't have crops any more. You had famines. You had major re-

FIGURE 3

400 Years of Sunspot Observation

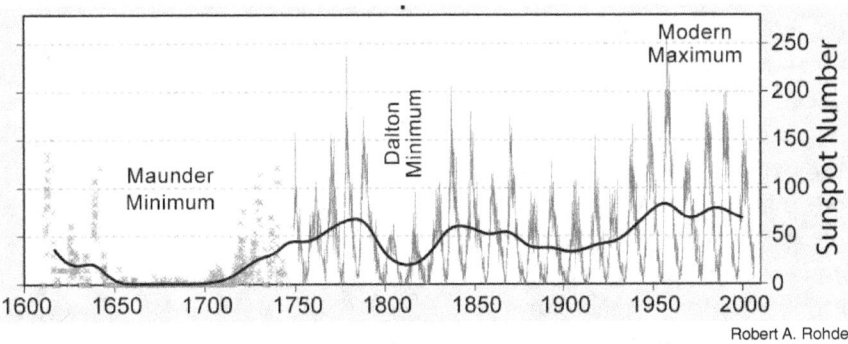

Robert A. Rohde

FIGURE 4

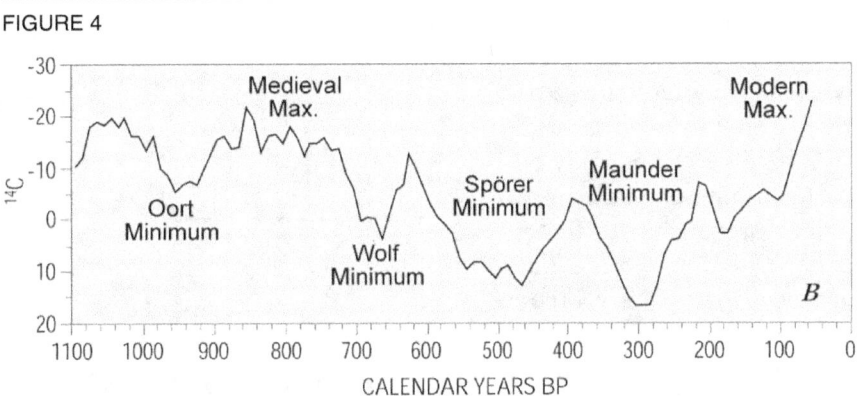

Solar activity over 1,100 years, measured by changes in production of carbon-14 in the atmosphere. More carbon-14 is produced by the increased galactic cosmic radiation the Earth experiences when the solar activity is low.

gions where rivers had run year-round without freezing, but now the rivers were completely freezing over. You had a very significant impact on society, on nations. Some of this is best documented in Northern Europe for that time period.

There is a growing concern that today, we are heading into a new "Maunder Minimum" period, when the Sun could become very weak. And we've seen that with the current solar cycle: It's less than half as intense as the previous predictions had expected. And the forecasts are, at this point, that the next cycle is going to be even weaker. So we're going into, potentially, a period of very low solar activity, which will have very serious effects on the Earth—much stronger effects than the claims about what will happen when you drive your car, in the whole "global warming" scare.

We've looked at the past 400 years; now, to put that in a larger perspective, let's look at the past 1,000 years (**Figure 4**). You can see, around 300 years ago, the Maunder Minimum, which was only one of several periods when the Sun became very weak. For an extended period of time—decades, 50 years—the Sun became very inactive. And for every one of these periods of low solar activity over the past 1,000 years, there is evidence of global cooling effects, regions of the planet getting dramatically colder, increased glaciation, increased ice flow—various evidence that the Earth as a whole got cooler in these periods of lower solar activity.

There's a recent study out of the Chinese Academy of Sciences, that showed that in certain regions of China, around Tibet, each of these periods of low solar activity corresponded to prolonged periods of drought.

So we have plenty of indications here that this is an immediate, serious concern that we have to be looking at and thinking about when we talk about the drought today.

FIGURE 5
The NAWAPA Region

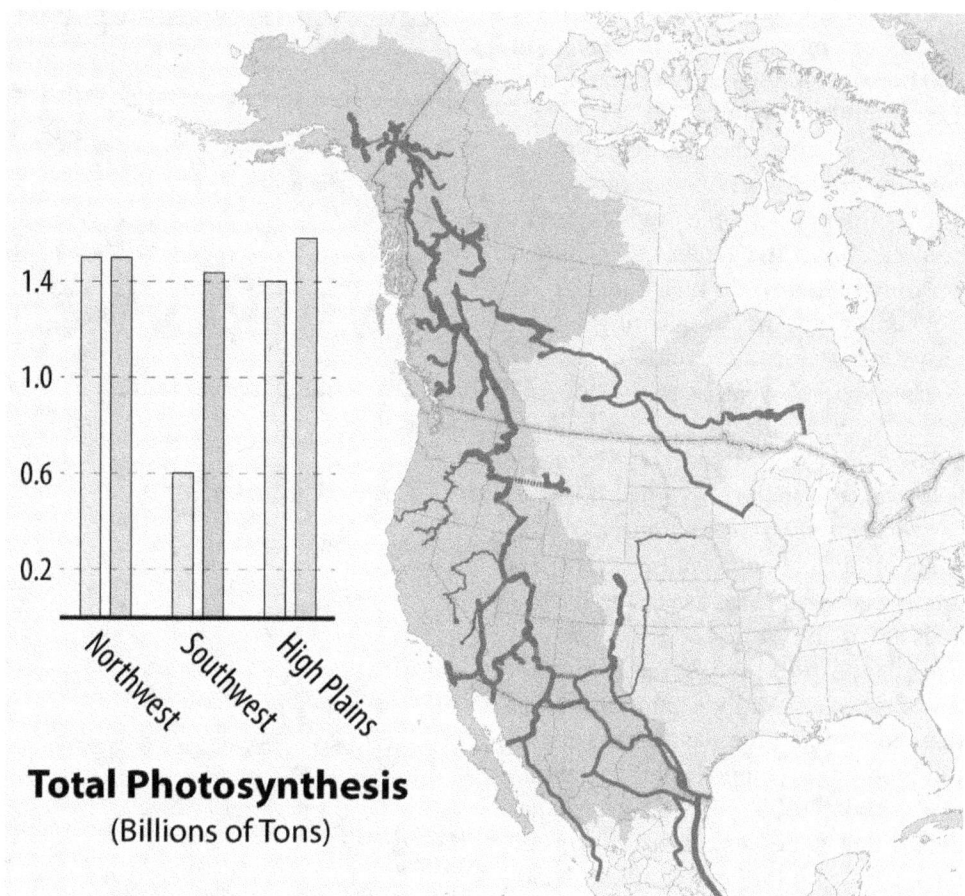

The North American Water and Power Alliance (NAWAPA) will counter the effects of solar-induced drought.

If we look at the activity of the Sun, if we look at the effects it has had in the past, and we look at where the Sun is going now—to a quiet, weaker phase—then we have no reason to assume that the water availability is going to return to the better days of 40, 50, or 60 years ago. If the West is going to survive and prosper; if California is going to produce food; if Texas is going to produce food; if the U.S. people are going to be fed, then mankind is going to have to abandon the green policy and take an active role in improving the conditions of the West.

Start Building NAWAPA Now

Figure 5 shows an illustration of the North American Water and Power Alliance project, which is a keystone project to save the western United States—a project that has been on the books for decades, to address the failure of the biosphere to distribute water in a sufficient way throughout the West. The natural conditions are such that you have a huge amount of precipitation, water, that falls in the very northern regions of the West: Alaska, British Columbia, Yukon Territory. A huge amount of water-flow there, but much of it goes completely unused, flowing right back into the ocean, without having a chance to participate in plant life, to participate in any type of biological system. Much of this water is pumped up, by evaporation by the Sun; dumped into the Northwest, and then runs right back into the ocean, completely unused.

If we are not insane greenies, and we recognize that mankind's obligation is to *improve* the territory of the planet, to improve the land, to improve the biosphere, to improve life, to make life better—then we recognize that this is an obvious, natural program: to

FIGURE 6

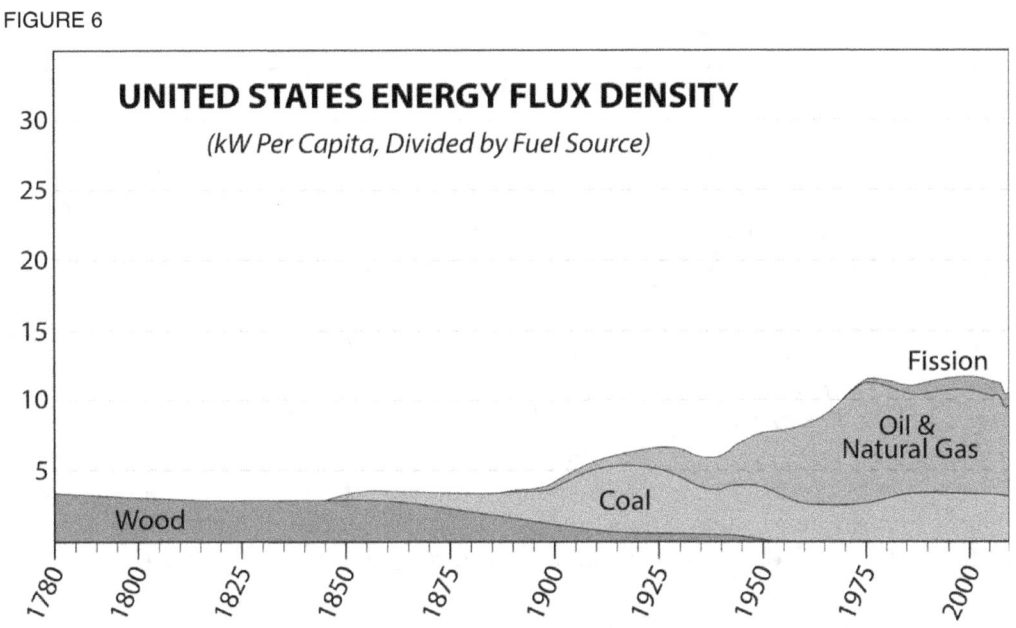

UNITED STATES ENERGY FLUX DENSITY

(kW Per Capita, Divided by Fuel Source)

Power per capita over the history of the United States, by power source.

poverty and improve the living conditions of the planet, mankind must, *today*, focus on thermonuclear fusion as the key driver for solving this crisis.

This can be illustrated in a number of ways, but **Figure 6**, which we've developed, puts the point very clearly. This is a history of the United States, measured by the energy use per capita. And you can see that the natural trajectory of progress has been a growth in energy use associated with transitions to higher and higher forms of energy: moving from a wood-based society to a coal-based society; moving from coal to oil and natural gas; moving beyond oil and natural gas.

This fracking policy is a total waste of economic activity: to burn natural gas for energy is insane at this point. We need natural gas for things like fertilizers; we need oil and gas for the petrochemical industry. We don't need them to get energy—we have nuclear fission available! But as you can see in this graphic, around 1970, with the takeover of the green policy, progress stopped! We stopped increasing our per-capita energy capability. We stopped increasing our energy-flux density. Fission power was suppressed. Fusion power was suppressed and never allowed to get started.

So we're at a crisis today that reflects the convergence of two key processes. One, the economic policy of the green, environmentalist paradigm that shut down progress, that stopped NAWAPA, that stopped the development of fission power, that stopped fusion power. And at the same time, we were seeing actual climate change driven by our Sun, as the Sun goes through its changes and fluctuations, which is ready to make life on Earth more difficult for any civilization that doesn't make the decisions to go with these programs of higher energy-flux density, fusion power, and major projects like NAWAPA....

These are the key economic programs needed immediately to save the nation.

bring water down from the Northwest to the central regions of the continent, down into the Southwest, and actually have a serious, long-term program to solve the water crisis and the drought conditions. And we're not talking about year-to-year fluctuations, but rather how can make sure that coming generations—your grandchildren—have a future in the western United States, that California and Texas continue to exist, continue to grow food, continue to develop and prosper and open up new land, and improve the territory.

This is the project you're going to need, this NAWAPA system. We've done extensive studies on this, consultations with experts. This is a real, live, active project that could be started immediately; that over the next 10-20 years, can begin to actually solve the real, long-term crisis associated with natural solar fluctuations, changes in solar activity, and their effects here on Earth....

Focus on Fusion Power

The one other thing I want to highlight, which is critical for this entire project, is the role of fusion power. That is, at this point, the future of mankind in the United States and in this planet generally. If we want projects like NAWAPA, if we want to be able to protect mankind against global cooling, to be able to deal with major fluctuations in the climate driven by changes in how active the Sun is; if we want to solve the problems of

Michael Steger

The Summer of 2014: An Anniversary, And an Opportunity To Mobilize

Michael Steger is running in the Democratic Party primary for Congress in California's 12th C.D. (San Francisco), against incumbent Nancy Pelosi. The primary election is on June 3.

This is an event that culminates and advances what Kesha Rogers and I have established as a unified campaign. What I want to touch on is, first, the strategic situation we confront today, because, although it's not the play itself, it is the stage on which this play will occur. And the play can either take two directions: It can either be a tragedy of human civilization, or it can be a triumph, and a fundamental transformation of human society. That's why Kesha and I are running these campaigns; that's why we're involved in this political fight; that's why we joined Mr. LaRouche, and this kind of idea of politics. Politics, not of issues, but of the fact that the human is something profound when it's human, when it's creative.

We are approaching a very important Summer. the Summer of 2014. It is the Summer that is now 100 years after the Summer of 1914: That means that over the course of the last hundred years, we have faced a policy of genocide and global warfare. For 100 years, there has been an ongoing level of destruction and of conflict, involving major nations, whether it's World War I, the economic destruction following, that led into World War II, which was essentially the same war; and then the ongoing threats of thermonuclear war, supposedly called the "Cold War" but of an ongoing contention: Will the human species survive? Or will it annihilate itself? For a hundred years this has been the threat and the destruction of nations, innumerable, across this planet.

Either we, today, change this paradigm, change the political course of the country, or we are not going to survive.

Now, the big reason for this, is Barack Obama.

He's a key driver in this threat of warfare today. We see it with the confrontations with Russia and Syria, and then in Ukraine. And the situation in Ukraine has *not* stepped back, the situation has escalated: More NATO troops, more destroyers headed into the Black Sea. A further breaking of diplomatic relations with the nations of Europe and Russia. Even a discontinuation of collaboration on scientific areas of advancement!

We are on a track, right now, similar to that of 1914: of war, but not a war of major artillery, or tanks, or airplanes—this is now a war of thermonuclear weapons. It is a war of extinction, and that is what we face.

Now, the problem is that there is a political disaster in this country, and the political disaster comes because of Barack Obama, the Wall Street groupings in both the Republican and Democratic Party. And the problem is that the Republicans, even the ones who might know

MichaelSteger.us

Michael Steger campaigns in San Francisco's Chinatown district.

better, have no economic solution. Their policies of free market/free trade are bankrupt, they've got no capability of addressing the drought crisis, the 25% plus levels of unemployment, an absolute breakdown in areas of manufacturing, engineering, or science, there's no commitment. No commitment to NASA, no commitment to fusion. And the rest of the Republican Party, namely its leadership, and most of its representation, is incredibly corrupted by Wall Street, and is pushing Obama further into an escalation of warfare. It's the Bush-Cheney faction, it's Torture, Inc.

This is the grouping Barack Obama protects; this is the grouping that put Barack Obama in office. It's a policy of Wall Street, it's a policy of bankruptcy of the United States, it's a policy of an escalation of warfare, the invasion of Libya, the threatened invasion of Syria, the protection of Cheney's torture policies.

And because of that commitment by Obama towards this fascist direction, we now see a split in the Democratic Party. And this is critical: to see a revival of the Franklin Roosevelt/John Kennedy legacy—which is not the "Democratic Party," because it by no means includes scum like Andrew Jackson, it's not the Democratic Party as a party institution. It represents a political tradition in the nation. It's the same as the tradition of Washington and Hamilton, it's the same one of Lincoln, it's the same one of Reagan.

You know, people in California, to this day, still love Ronald Reagan; many people in the United States do—why? Because he identified himself with the tradition of Franklin Roosevelt, and he broke from the Democratic Party because of traitors like Truman, or Carter, in his policies. And people became "Reagan Democrats," because they were patriots of a country. And the problem today is, where is that Democratic Party? Where is that American political tradition?

This is the crisis that we face.

The Green Fascist Agenda

Now, I can give people a clearer sense of what's happening in California, but what Ben Deniston laid out [in the preceding speech] is the critical policy orientation: We have to have a full-scale orientation against this green program. Take, for example, the green program here in California, and in Texas, and across the country: It's targeting the Dakotas right now, this policy of fracking. You need natural gas for chemicals! You need natural gas to heat your stove, it's better than electric ovens or electric stoves. But you don't need to burn natural gas for electricity! But why are we doing it? In California, that's *all* we do! We don't use wind power or solar power for much of any anything. It's a small percentage of what we consume. The reason we depend on natural gas, is because of this green agenda: We're "saving" the environment, by burning natural gas: we're "protecting" our atmosphere from carbon dioxide pollution. We're basically starving the trees!

But that's the policy, to save the environment: Burn natural gas, lower your carbon emissions. But how do you get natural gas? To get that natural gas, you now have to take, in an area of extensive drought west of the Mississippi, in places like Texas and California, especially, you have a program of taking precious water, combining that with a cocktail of chemicals, and pumping that into your land. People say, well, it doesn't affect the land … that much. Yeah, the first six months of the year won't destroy the land-area, completely. The Earth is actually fairly resilient. But do it for five years, and ten years, and 20 years, and what you end up doing is destroying your land and your water area! You end up destroying the actual, very precious resources, that the future of mankind depends upon. Which is not just the land and water supply as they are, but the ability to commit to transforming that land and water supply to be far more productive than it naturally is. That's mankind's potential.

So the fracking program is to harvest that natural gas, supposedly to save the environment, when in reality, we're destroying the land and water supply we're using every day. And we're consuming the precious water we don't have, to get the natural gas.

So the environmental agenda is *not* anything to save the environment! It is an outright destruction of the environment, in every possible way! To eliminate and shut down the ability of the human population to survive.

But what is the real green agenda? Because the real green agenda isn't simply the "atmosphere" question. It isn't simply the endangered species, to save a small fish in the Sacramento Delta. The real green agenda was the shutdown of nuclear power and development. Because if you had nuclear power, you wouldn't have fracking; if you had nuclear power, to the extent that Presidents like Eisenhower and Kennedy had put forward, you would have commercial fusion today. And that's the future of the country, that's the future of the human species.

Revive the FDR-JFK Tradition

So the question today, is a return to the Franklin Roosevelt and John Kennedy tradition. And we're beginning to get a break of this nature, as you see with Sen. [Dianne] Feinstein, you've seen outright the contention with this administration; you see people like Rep. Adam Schiff, who's also from California, southern California. And this is a critical juncture, because if we don't make a break today, politically, instead of Kesha and I—just look at the other candidates the Democratic Party is running! There's one now in the Hudson Valley, who is run and sponsored entirely by Wall Street, Facebook, this nasty CIA/NSA operation. That's what the Democratic Party is pushing in other candidates!

Creative Commons/Gordon

The Stevens Creek Reservoir in Cupertino, Calif., Feb. 6, 2014. The state's drought is the worst in recorded state history, and some towns will be completely without water this Summer.

So you people have to begin to decide: Are you going to go with a Wall Street-sponsored fascist program, which both parties look to for funding, because nobody else will give them any money? Who would give money to the Democratic and Republican Party? Nobody does! They call them, and they get yelled at, because no one would want to give money to these political parties.

These political parties are bankrupt in a large degree, but there is a break. If you look at the people who joined Adam Schiff from Glendale, from southern California, on this letter to Obama on the question of the CIA—. Schiff wrote a letter, demanding that Obama release this CIA torture report. And what does the torture report document? It documents that treason has occurred since President Clinton and his Presidency was sabotaged by the Al Gore faction in the Democratic Party, this green, Wall Street faction, by a nasty grouping of Republicans, and by British networks, people like Ambrose Evans-Pritchard, who covered this for the London papers. And they destroyed Clinton's Presidency, and they shut down the Glass-Steagall legislation, and they brought in 15 years of treason, treason that you now see documented in this 6,000-page report—that we were *torturing* people, that we were committing war crimes, wars of aggression based on false intelligence and lies. We were sponsoring a Wall Street coup in the bailout program. This is an existential threat to the country, and Barack Obama and his administration have been covering it up the entire time!

So now, you've got people fighting on it, and a lot of them come from California, because the state is dying. And this is the break we have to now use, as a wedge, and this is the leadership that Kesha and I represent, and the other candidates that we're [the LaRouche movement] running, because there's a chance to now break open, not the Democratic Party, but a revival of a true American political tradition. And that's the essence of the fight.

California Is Being Destroyed

Now, take a look at the drought in California, because it's critical; it's critical now, for actual communities in the state and small towns. There are literally towns that will be out of water by this Summer. They will have *no water at all.*

This is a state dominated by the Democratic party—the Democratic Party has absolute control, in any real significant sense, of the statehouse, the governorship, all of the institutions. What is the Democratic Party's approach to the drought? Who does the drought affect? It affects the rural areas, it affects farm areas: California's Central Valley is the most productive food area in the world! You can grow things here that you can't grow anywhere else. You can grow *everything* here that you can grow anywhere else, and you can grow it three or four times bigger. This is a food productive area that's a model of human intervention to develop our resources, and to improve the society in which we live, for generations.

And the Democratic Party in California is letting

California Gov. Gerry Brown signs a State of Emergency proclamation on Jan. 17, 2014, directing state officials to "prepare" for drought conditions. But meaningful emergency action has not been taken.

that Valley *die*! They're letting cities go without water, entire areas go without water, entire orchards go without water; orchards are getting ripped up. Nearly a million acres of land are going fallow this year alone. And if the drought continues, it'll get worse, because your farmworkers, or the skilled labor that can pick the vegetables, and fruits, and nuts, that 30-40% of our population depend upon, are going to have to go somewhere else. They're going to have to go back to Mexico, under the reign of terror of drug cartels, *backed by this administration*, which is destroying an agricultural capability.

The same thing is being done to research facilities in this state, areas that were leaders of development of fusion energy and technology, like Lawrence Livermore Labs, or Lawrence Berkeley, are getting gutted. JPL [the Jet Propulsion Laboratory], Obama shut down flagship programs for NASA: There are no more projects to Mars, such as Curiosity. Those projects have been cut. There is no more fusion funding! Lawrence Livermore Labs has the National Ignition Facility. It's a major area of breakthrough in fusion research—but they're not funding fusion research there, now; it's just an investigation of what happens when a thermonuclear bomb explodes. It's weapons research now, that's it—*under Obama!*

So this state is getting dismantled.

Gov. Jerry Brown and the Democratic Party in California have heralded a great economic recovery. A re-

covery of what? The state has 25%-plus unemployment. In youth unemployment, among those 25 and younger, it's 40%-plus! It's like southern Europe!

The state is 49th in education, where it used to be number one. We used to have the best public school system in the country: university research facilities, college education programs, public schools. It had research, it had technology, it had aerospace, it had agriculture, advanced infrastructure. That's the climate by which you educate a younger generation to become productive, to be optimistic, but you've torn it all down!

And now the state's dying. Literally, you have towns which will become ghost towns, in a matter of months.

Now, the Democratic Party's approach is a water bond, which may build a dam or a new reservoir in the next ten years. Similar proposals are coming out of Congress. It might have worked ten years ago, but it won't do much to save the towns and cities today.

The other approach they're taking, is discussion of how you can take a little bit of water from Peter to give a little bit of water to Paul, who will have none in a few months. But if there's no long-term commitment to either of their survival, then you have a Hobbesian world of each against all, and there's no real compassion or development of society: That's a breakdown of civilization.

The bigger problem, and this is where people don't fight, because these are good intentions on some level, but where's the fight? It's because the Wall Street-pimped media in California is willing to say, "We don't need to grow food in California! You don't need to grow food in the Western states! Just let it go under." You know, "New Orleans shouldn't have been built: That was the big problem, with the hurricane [Katrina]. Why did we build a city so close to the ocean?" "Why do we build farmland in an arid area?" Well, it happens to be that plants like arid climate! They like the rich soils of the Central Valley: We just brought water to them. And what NAWAPA does, is bring water from where it can't be used, to where it can be used the most, in the arid and rich soils of the Southwest.

But you've got journalists and media today in California and across the country, saying, we don't need to grow food. We'll just live off the backs of cheap labor in other countries, or we'll just let people die. We'll let your food prices go up (as they already are); we'll cut your incomes, we'll steal your savings accounts; we'll take away your Social Security.

And people say, "What d'ya mean, 'genocide'! What d'ya mean, 'British Empire'?"

Well, what's happening? This *is* a genocide policy! It is is not a policy of the United States, not of its real political tradition, not of its patriots. It's a policy of its *traitors*, who work for this kind of an empire policy, and empire program.

We're Going for Victory

And this is the fight, because this is what we have to break open. We have to break open this commitment. What John Kennedy wanted to do, what Robert Kennedy wanted to do, what Lyndon LaRouche has been fighting for, for a very long time, is the revival of this political tradition. This is what makes us human, in a real sense, because we sacrifice with an idea that we're not going to fight for small gains in a losing battle, or a losing war. We're going to go for a victory in the war, because that's worth living for.

Mr. LaRouche has written a recent paper, which takes up this real American political tradition, a true American political tradition; and he gets at a problem which precedes, and is actually the cause of why we were so susceptible to accepting a century of warfare. And after a hundred years of warfare, and under this administration, and under the cowardice of our political leadership, we're now facing a thermonuclear war, a war of extinction. But in the earlier part of our century, we lost a sense of what it meant to be human, we lost a sense of creativity.

It was replaced with a cult of mathematics. Why is that so important?

Because, how do you actually measure something? If you want to measure an economy, how do you measure it? With a ruler? With a dollar? They measure agriculture today by the financial value it has. That's insanity! That's an expression of how extreme this has become—not by bushels or by weight, but by dollars.

The question of how we measure something gets at the essence of what makes us human, because it's not your brain that measures, it's not what you see, it's the

Creative Commons/Russ Allison Loar

Give these guys a job! Build NAWAPA! California's youth unemployment is at the levels of southern Europe, and will get worse as the impact of the nation's failed economic policies worsens.

process. What people today see in this economy, what they see with Obama, and why there's 80% rejection of this Presidency, is because the process they see is downward—faster and faster! Each day, you find out it's gotten worse, and it's getting worse faster than you thought before. And that's scares people. They see a Presidency running into collision course with a thermonuclear power. They see the bankruptcy of a financial system, and no one doing anything about it. Not one prosecution! Not one banker in jail!

Because we don't measure things by objects or by numbers. What we measure them with is the human mind. And where is the human mind? How big is it? Quantify it. You use your mind in that political process, you use your mind to measure the growth of your child's creative potential. But the mind doesn't have a sensual characteristic; it measures a process, it measures a development characteristic. And the problem is, that we don't have that in the culture today; it's been ripped out!

Why don't people see this world war coming? Why don't people see this economic bankruptcy? Why don't they have the courage to address it? Because they've been reduced to a quantified characteristic, to sense-perception, to just simply what they see. Or they're willing to accept arguments that are very simplistic:

"No, no, it could never happen, because no one would ever let that happen; they wouldn't let a world war happen." Well, it's been a hundred years of world war! They just haven't let thermonuclear extinction happen. But because it's never happened before, means it's not going to happen again? Or it's not going to happen tomorrow?

I think we have to go back to this question: You have to fight for that sense of creativity, and we have to uproot this cult of mathematics. If you take a look at San Francisco's economy, which is a great herald of "recovery" in California: It's a Potemkin Village! You've got these fronts of so-called "technology companies," but they don't do anything! You walk down the street, you look at them: They play ping-pong! They play pinball machines! They're not producing anything! They make video games for your phone! This is not an economy, these are little cults! They live and eat and play in these same buildings. It's not an economy, it's not a technological center, it's not a driver for the economy of the United States. What an absurdity! Silicon Valley is a driver for the U.S. economy?

The "recovery" in California came from Wall Street's propped-up bubbles, or Twitter! And the so-called tax revenues in California gave it a recovery. And now, because of this drought, because of the shutdown of agriculture—which is really the number-one production in California—because of the shutdown in scientific research at places like the national labs, the state's going to go into a massive deficit. Because that Wall Street bubble can't sustain itself, and Wall Street knows it, London knows it, and they're going for war.

People have to get a sense of this! They have to clear away all of the distractions and say, "This is the reality, this is what defines the political fight this Summer." We've got to break open this real, American political tradition. And if we do that, if we fight now, if Kesha makes a break in Texas on May 27, that can change the entire political discussion in this country. But we've got to *fight* for it! Because everything's at stake, and our enemy on Wall Street and in London, they know it, they know we're coming out for them! Because they don't produce anything. If we expose that, people will rally behind these policies. They don't believe this green agenda.

And so this is the fight of the unified campaign.

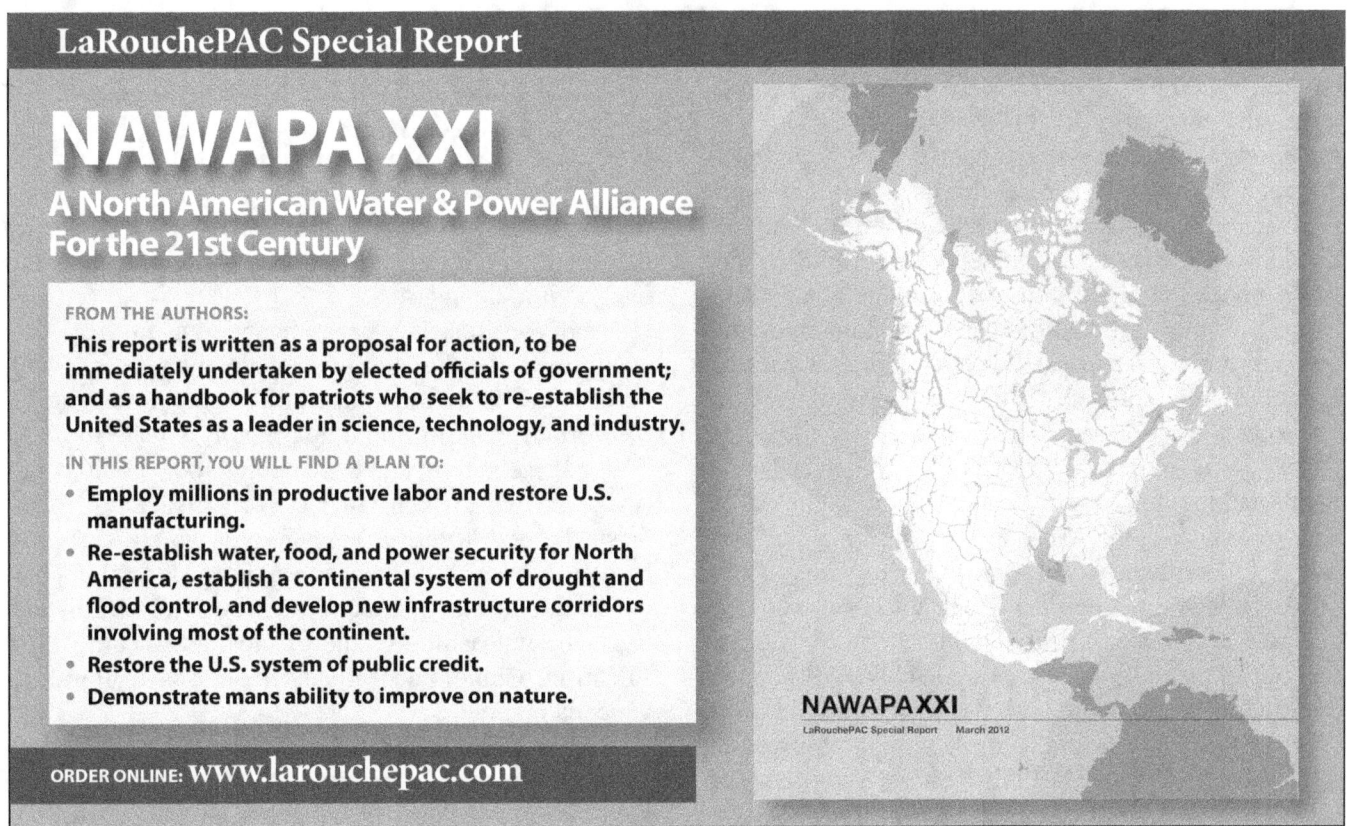

Saving the Nation by Returning to the Policies of Lincoln, FDR, and Kennedy

Kesha Rogers is a candidate in the May 27 runoff election in Texas, for the Democratic nomination for Senate.

I will continue in this trajectory of the composition that has already been set forth, by giving the marching orders of how we are going to go about defining the return to the true American political tradition. And first of all, I have to say this: It's going to require a rising up in the population of once and for all coming to understand what your true human identity must be comprised of and expressed in. And I think that we can really take our inspiration by understanding, first and foremost, what is this uniquely American political tradition?

You can look at three unique periods in our nation's history that I want to define, where the conception of the new frontier for mankind really took off. One, under the leadership of President Abraham Lincoln, with the Transcontinental Railway; two, under the leadership of President Franklin Roosevelt, with the Tennessee Valley Authority; and three, under the leadership of President John F. Kennedy, with the continuation of the Franklin Roosevelt policies, and the American System tradition, with what he had set into motion with the Apollo mission.

What they represent, those three achievements, is what is going to be required for the survival of the United States and moving toward a new frontier for our nation, and for us to take the leadership of impacting the entire world, of giving the world a vision, once again.

And that's one thing that Michael Steger and I understand, that our political opponents don't—and neither one of the political parties actually has any conception that the population needs a mission; we need visionary leaders who are going to actually say, we can, once and for all, get rid of this imperial system of free trade, or globalization, of green environmentalist stu-

EIRNS

Kesha Rogers represents the visionary leadership needed to rid the U.S. of the imperial system of free trade, globalization, and green stupidity.

pidity, and of Wall Street corruption, that that is not the basis by which our nation and the progress of our great republic was founded. And anyone who is opposing that identity, of our true American System, is not fit to lead or fit to be in office.

And you look at what is happening, in these two states in particular, because, what we're expressing here, today, is that the state of Texas and the state of California, working in collaboration, will be the new TVAs of the nation; and this is going to be done by our two campaigns, which Michael and I are leading, to unleash the new frontier for mankind, which is already being expressed by what Ben Deniston [see above] laid out in the North American Water and Power Alliance XXI, the unleashing of the greatest advancements of scientific, technological advancements, agricultural advancements.

Why is it that the state of Texas, one of the most productive, industrial, agricultural, scientific states in the nation, is now facing the worst drought in history?

Just a few weeks ago, on March 18, there was a major dust storm that blew over the area of Lubbock, Texas. Just recently, you have an increase of about 46 counties and growing throughout the state of Texas, which are running out of water! Texas is running out of water, because we have a Wall Street and British puppet in the White House, Barack Obama, who is not addressing the concerns and the needs of the fact that you have people starving, in the state of Texas and across the United States.

College Students Are Starving

We just had a report in, today, that you have young people who are furthering their education in college, across the nation, who are starving, who do not have food! They don't have food, because we're bailing out the Wall Street bankers and the corruption of the bail-in policy, taking away people's deposits, taking away people's livelihoods, and leaving them to die. Young people trying to further their education, are having to go to food banks. When Obama was first elected, in 2008, there were four food banks at universities and colleges throughout the United States; now there are going on 121 food banks at the universities and colleges! How do you leave your young people starving? We're doing the same thing to our military veterans. We're putting them out of house, home, starving them.

And there is a simple solution to dealing with all of this: You bankrupt these bastards on Wall Street, tell them they will not have the right to the lives of the American people. You say, "Glass-Steagall *now*!" That's the only solution. If we don't get Glass-Steagall through, we're not going to be able to solve this crisis. If we don't immediately implement the policies toward an advancement in the highest forms of scientific and technological development, so that we can put millions of people back to work in productive jobs, we're not going to survive this.

And as Michael laid out, the threat is very clear, the strategic situation is at a crossroads, and people have to stop playing party politics. You have some corrupt Wall Street Bushites, who are sitting there, saying, "Oh don't touch Obama. Keep on messing up, Obama, because it's looking good for us. We're going to get our Wall Street money, and we're going to win an election on the backs of the lives of the population."

We've got something for you: If we are in the middle of thermonuclear war, there will be no election, for you Wall Street Republicans, or your money!

So, we have to stop playing party politics here. Democrats have to get off the Bush plantation here in Texas, and across the nation, and actually redefine and take back their commitment to this uniquely American political idea of what was represented by President Abraham Lincoln, President John F. Kennedy, and President Franklin Roosevelt.

Now, when President Franklin Roosevelt defined the policy for the Tennessee Valley Authority, you take that as a case example. The Tennessee Valley was very backward in education policy; you had the flooding of the rivers in the whole Tennessee Valley area; you had a collapse in agricultural production; and what did we do? We went into this area and we transformed it, with the most advanced, agricultural, scientific, productive capability that the nation had seen, probably since the development of the Transcontinental Railway system, which Abraham Lincoln had set in place.

The American System

But one thing I want to point out about all of these three unique achievements, you know what they opposed? They opposed this British imperial system of free trade, globalization, which is against everything that our American Republic represented. These three achievements were the embodiment of our American Republic, and our American political tradition. And so, you can't have these three achievements, with the policy of Wall Street bailouts and Wall Street corruption. Wall Street was not leading the charge under the Presidency of Abraham Lincoln. Abraham Lincoln told Wall Street to take a hike, as he initiated the policy of Alexander Hamilton's credit system program, which is our Constitution. Which is our uniquely American tradition.

And so, today, when people say, "Well, we don't have enough food to eat, we can't feed our population, we don't have an adequate water supply, but we don't have the money to take care of all of this." Well, how do you have the money to bail out trillions of dollars in speculative gambling activity for the Wall Street financial interests, but you don't have the money to make sure our people have food to eat? You don't have the money to make sure that we can feed our troops? That's insanity.

And so anyone who would dare challenge that and say that we can go on—especially Democrats—defending and protecting this President, is insane! This is complete insanity: This President has to go. He has to be impeached, now. We need a full-scale mobilization in the recovery program for our nation. The recovery program is clearly defined. And if you look at what we've experienced, here in the state of Texas, just to kind of give you a sense: I've been going, along with my team for the U.S. Senate, all across the state. First of all, you have to ask yourself, in the state of Texas, we have the lowest voter turnout of all 50 states. Why is that? People—what are they voting for? What is our mission in this nation? You have 500,000 Democrats coming out, 1.3 million Republicans coming out to vote [in Texas], you know, the tight-knit party establishment, and that's the way they want to keep it—until *we* go out there, and we organize the population. There's 13 million people that are registered to vote in this state! So that should tell you something: Are we going to instill in our population a sense that we are fighting for them?

National Geographic channel videograb

In his speech at the Brooks Aerospace Medical Division in San Antonio Nov. 21, 1963, President Kennedy called on Americans to "test the unknown and the uncertain in every phase of human endeavor." His voice was forever silenced the next day in Dallas.

Taking the Fight to the Streets

I can tell you, what we're doing with my campaign, and with Michael's campaign in San Francisco, is, we're taking this fight to the street. We're going out there, and we're talking to farmers, and we're talking to veterans, and we're talking to political activists; we're talking to those we're meeting on the streets every single day, who have given up on the political system, who have said, "I was once proud to be in the tradition of the John F. Kennedy/Franklin Roosevelt legacy, what happened to that?" Well, because you went to sleep, and you let the Wall Street control take over. And now it's time for you to wake up, and now it's time for you to say, "I'm not going to turn a blind eye, but I'm going to, as a citizen of this republic, *do* something to change the conditions of this nation." And that requires taking immediate action, now.

When John F. Kennedy, 30 years after the anniversary of the TVA, went to visit Muscle Shoals in the Tennessee Valley and spoke there, one of the things he said,

is that the TVA will never be finished. There will *always* be new frontiers to conquer. And this was May of 1963; it was about six months later, in November of 1963, that John F. Kennedy was actually right here in San Antonio, Texas, the day before his assassination. He was here, speaking at the Aerospace Medical Health Center, and this is what he said:

"For more than three years I have spoken about the New Frontier. This is not a partisan term, and it is not the exclusive property of Republicans or Democrats. It refers, instead, to this nation's place in history, to the fact that we do stand on the edge of a great new era, filled with both crisis and opportunity, an era to be characterized by achievement and by challenge. It is an era which calls for action and for the best efforts of all those who would test the unknown and the uncertain in every phase of human endeavor. It is a time for pathfinders and pioneers...."

And that's the moment we find ourselves in today. We're in a new era, which poses challenges and opportunity. And you think about those opportunities which are being denied us. Today is the anniversary of the flight of the first man in space, Russian cosmonaut Yuri Gagarin. And you think about what those opportunities set into motion: A month after Yuri Gagarin flew into space, you had Alan Shepard, the first American to go into space. And that was a signification of what the United States represented, with our commitment toward peaceful relations among nations.

Obama: Shutting Down Our Space Program

What is Obama doing today? Not only are we shutting down our manned space program, we're shutting down our science-driver programs in the funding of NASA and the development of the mission toward unleashing new endeavors in space, and understanding how that's going to have an impact on the advancement of the progress of mankind. But we're saying, "No, no more working or collaboration with Russia!" Even during the periods of heightened tensions between the United States and Russia, we would *never* have taken down our collaboration in terms of our space program. With the Apollo-Soyuz mission, we were still working with these nations, we were still working with Russia, we were still working on the advancement of scientific progress.

Under President John F. Kennedy, you think about the fact that it was in the 1960s, thirty years after FDR's TVA program, that the TVA had the most advanced scientific achievements: You had the increase in nuclear power; but just a decade later, you had the green environmentalist genocide agenda that came in, and took all of that down, and started the policy in the 1970s, to move away, as Michael was saying, from those achievements that had already been set into motion.

So the reality which we face right now, is people have to have an understanding of the expression of what this uniquely American political achievement and identity is, so that you will know what to fight for. I find it interesting, there was an article that came out on my campaign, that says, "Kesha Rogers, you can't trust her, she's always smiling and laughing." Well, if you understand what our unique identity as Americans is and as human beings is, that we're not slaves to a British Empire, that we're not slaves to a Bush plantation and George Bush and Dick Cheney—Dick Cheney, with his insane fracking policy, fracking up all of Texas and California—that we have a system, defined by our Constitution, defined by the commitment of great achievers and leaders, such as John Quincy Adams, such as Abraham Lincoln, and others, and going back to the American credit system of Alexander Hamilton, if you understand this, then you know how to fight, and you are optimistic! And you can actually understand, that we can defeat these bastards. And that's what we intend to do.

So, as we go out and we talk to people, we have to make clear: The threat of thermonuclear war is on the table, and has to be taken off. The only way it's going to be taken off is, this President goes out; we're going to get Glass-Steagall through now; we need a credit policy to investment in the most productive development of our nation. And we can start with the state of Texas.

As I go around to the different areas in Texas—you have places like Barnhart and others, that are dried up and depleted of water, because we're fracking in these areas, when we should be going for advancement in the increase in our production and energy-flux density. We need nuclear power. I just visited one of the only two nuclear power facilities here in the state of Texas, just a couple of days ago, the Comanche Peak nuclear facility. And you think about, you have that one, and then you have the South Texas Project.

We need a total advancement of nuclear power, in a fusion economy, and we need that so that we can shut down this insane green agenda, and we can actually move forward with achieving the accomplishments of what's necessary to provide a standard of living for our population, which will increase, not just the energy-flux density, but will increase the productive powers of our population.

You Have To Have a Vision

The North American Water And Power Alliance (NAWAPA), this program will provide *millions* of productive jobs immediately. And we're not just talking about putting people back to work in makeshift work. What we're talking about is a whole transformation of your nation's physical economy. You can't start by talking about a localized effort of how we're going to deal with Texas, and how we're going to deal with California. You have to have a vision, and these two states, being the leaders in our nation and the republic, the two most advanced, productive states, scientific states—these states probably compromise something like 20% of the nation's population, or more. You have most of the food production coming from here, in the states of Texas and California. Once you lose that, you're going to lose the nation!

So people have to look at these states, which represent, as I said before, the new frontier for this. And we can go about achieving that, if people would free themselves, and decide that they're going to fight. And they're going to fight, not just in their own interests, but they're going to fight for the interests of those who are yet unborn.

Thank you, very much.

EIREconomics

A NATIONAL EMERGENCY

Impeachable Crimes: Fracking Is Genocide—Shut It Down!

by Marcia Mery Baker and Paul Gallagher

April 22—The killer shortage of food and energy supplies brought about by drought, fracking (hydraulic fracturing), and Obama-backer multi-billionaire Warren Buffett's financial manipulation of vital transportation infrastructure, must be reversed by decisive action from lawmakers: Impeach Obama. Stop fracking. Sack Buffett. Use Federal powers to ensure that vital supplies have access to transportation and to push through the development of the fusion power-driven North American Water and Power Alliance (NAWAPA XXI). The energy-flux density of our national economy must rise with technological advances, not sink into Hell with "green" Wall Street practices.

The fact of the extreme drought in the Southwest is now widely publicized; but the extent of today's crisis includes the fact that in Texas, California, and elsewhere in the dry Western states, the "Great Fracking Oil & Gas Boom" is sucking up scarce water for wells; using up limited railroad capacity to haul oil; using up pipeline capacity to convey gas products—especially propane—for export, all while domestic users go short, and pay to the hilt. Chaos is spreading.

In the Northern Plains, the 2013 harvest of wheat, corn, beans, and other farm commodities is overflowing storage capacity, for lack of rail shipment to move out the product. Meantime, next to no fertilizer has been shipped in for Spring planting. Food processors are on a go-slow. Warren Buffett's Berkshire Hathaway Corp. controls the largest railroad network serving the entire area, and has huge investments in the companies that are "fracking" oil and ship-

Creative Commmons/Joshua Doubek

Fracking by Halliburton in the Bakken Shale Basin. The company was formerly owned by Dick Cheney, who greased the skids to exempt fracking technology from rational environmental oversight ("the Halliburton loophole").

FIGURE 1
Lower 48 States Shale Plays

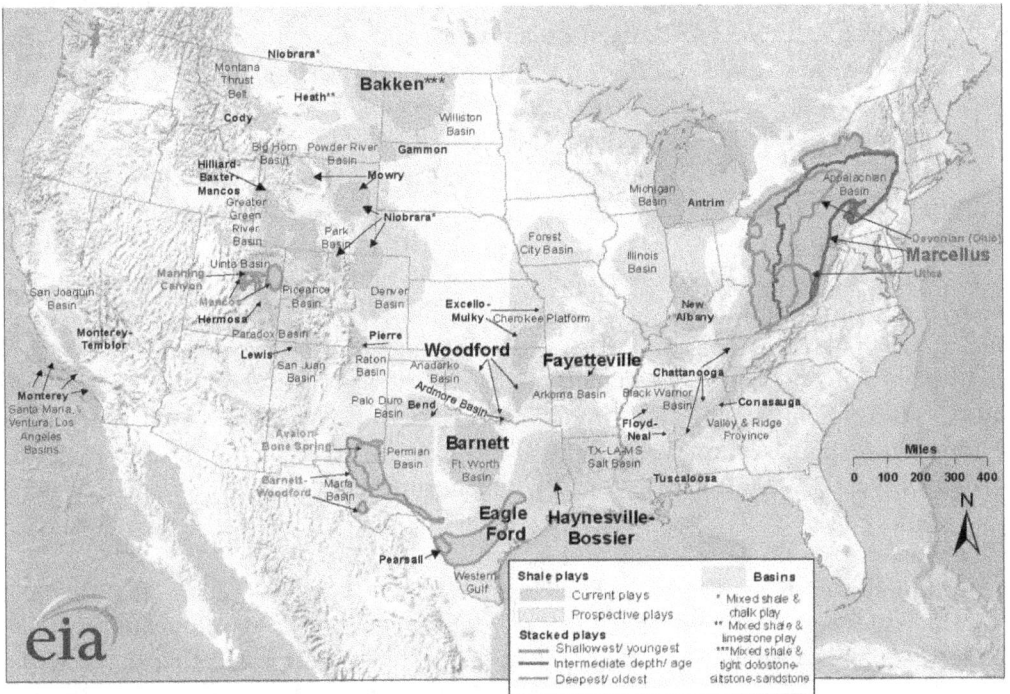

Rep. Kevin Cramer were the prime sponsors), passed only six days earlier. This was the Bureau of Land Management Streamlining Act, S. 244 and H.R. 767. It created new BLM offices in North Dakota and Montana for the purpose of rubber-stamping and fast-tracking permits for fracking on public lands in the Bakken Shale Basin.

This is no party politics issue. Obama is a continuation of the infamous Dick Cheney Energy Task Force perspective, of doing whatever the Wall Street/London oil and gas network demands.

Congress is hereby informed: If you are backing fracking—whether because of your fantasies of energy independence, facing down Russia, or plain old pay-off and corruption—you are in line for impeachment.

ping it and all its precursors in rail cars by the hundreds of thousands.

From near zero five years ago, "fracking oil" is now shipped at the rate of 1 million barrels/day from the North Dakota Bakken Shale and other basins, largely on Buffett's Burlington Northern Santa Fe (BNSF) Railroad.

This process, destroying communities and threatening farmers and local dealers with ruin, now constitutes a food supply crisis, and national emergency. The entire process must be stopped. Use of Federal injunction and related measures are called for, in particular to remove Warren Buffett from corporate office at once. Start criminal prosecution.

Fracking is a hallmark Obama policy:

• In March 2012, Obama signed Executive Order 13604, by which Obama created a Bakken Federal Executive Group to "find ways to facilitate the development of oil and gas resources in the booming Bakken Formation." The Deputy Interior Secretary assigned to head this group said, "By coordinating across the many Federal agencies involved in the Bakken region, we are able to offer a better process for industry."

• On Dec. 26, 2013, Obama signed a Republican-originated bill (North Dakota's Sen. John Hoeven and

I. Upper Midwest States Crisis

As of the April planting season in the Upper Midwest, chaos prevails in agriculture, directly arising from the Bakken Shale oil fracking operations and oil-train shipments. BNSF Railroad dominates the rail service in this region, with Canadian Pacific Railway second. BNSF is wholly owned by Buffett's Berkshire Hathaway. Buffett is carrying out, with the Obama Administration, the fracking/tight oil "boom" policy of the British financial empire.

The severity of the resulting agriculture crisis was presented on April 10, by Northern Plains states agriculture leaders, to a Washington, D.C. hearing of the Surface Transportation Board of the Transportation Department. The STB then issued the unusual directive on April 15, *to order BNSF to make special fertilizer shipments,* and provide its plan to do so by April 18; and "to report their plans to ensure delivery of fertilizer shipments for Spring planting of U.S. crops, and, beginning April 25, 2014, to provide weekly status reports for six weeks regarding fertilizer delivery over their respective networks."

The STB directive stated, "Given the immediate need for fertilizer to meet repidly approaching planting deadlines, and the potential long-lasting and widespread effects of missing those deadlines, the Board" has taken its decision.

Testimony at the hearing provided horror stories about the consequences of Buffett's oil-rail bonanza. Brian Schanilec, a North Dakota fifth-generation farmer and president of the Forest River Bean Co., said, "We have crops we cannot sell; we have discounts [loss in prices received for their product—ed.] that are historical. And now, we won't have to plant half our acres, because we can't get our crops to market. This is the biggest crossroads in our history. We cannot secure enough fertilizer to plant our crops this year." (Video of hearing at www.stb.dot.gov)

Fertilizer. Farmer cooperatives in the Dakotas have been unable to receive or line up timely shipments of fertilizer for Spring planting. The state needs some 800,000 tons of nitrogen-based fertilizer each year, and it isn't there. Some cooperatives have even quit pre-selling fertilizer, because they can't line up delivery.

Corn. North Dakota Farmers Union president Mark Watne told the April 10 hearing, "We have heard from co-op managers who believe that 85% of this year's corn crop [2013] is still in either on-farm or warehouse storage. They also believe there is a good chance that this year's crop will not be moved before the new crop has to go into storage. To take this even one step further, there is a growing fear that cooperatives will not be able to get access to the fertilizer needed to plant this year's crop."

South Dakota Agriculture Secretary Lucas Lentsch told the hearing that at least 11,000 railcars have been delayed for shipment of grain. The elevators are having problems with spoilage; Many cannot accept any more grain for storage. Gov. Dennis Daugaard has warned that his state could become the world's "warehouse for grain," if the rail system isn't changed.

Wheat. Shipments out are running at least a month behind in the northern wheat states. Minnesota Grain and Feed Association director Robert Zelenka told the STB hearing, "One of our biggest concerns looking forward is the likelihood of going into the Fall's harvest with elevators close to full of grain and no freight to ship it. This will create some major problems, which will back onto farm storage and harvest delays."

Over the border, in Canada, some 6 million tons of wheat have backed up and can't move. Farmers are taking losses. Many can't sell. The Canadian government is entertaining a national rules change, to allow more interconnection of Canadian and U.S. rail services by the U.S-headquartered BNSF, which is already failing on the U.S. side of the border!

Sugar. American Crystal Sugar, based outside Fargo, N.D., announced earlier this year that because of lack of rail service, it will scale back output (from sugar beets) at three of its plants, because of running out of storage space, waiting for rail cars.

Propane. Shortage of propane supplies and hyper-inflated prices have wreaked havoc in the Upper Midwest since December, and for reasons parallel to the Buffett oil-rail domination: The U.S. gas pipeline system, of which Buffett is a foremost owner, is serving cartel export and other interests above agro-industrial and public needs.

The Upper Midwest states, as well as New England and the South, were slammed this Winter, with propane scarcity and spiking prices. It's still that way. At the STB hearing, Minnesota grains leader Robert Zelenka spoke about "the recurring problem with the movement and placement of propane for this Fall's grain-drying needs and home heating."

Over the past 18 months, the Obama Administration lifted restrictions against exports of certain Natural Gas Liquids (NGLs) including propane. Given that the world "market" price was much higher than the domestic, the London/Wall Street cartels shipped it abroad. Exports of propane and propylene have increased 5.5 times in the past two years, tripling in the last year alone. In 2013, more than 20% of all U.S. propane was exported, way up from 5% in 2008.

On Feb. 7, the Federal Energy Regulatory Commission (FERC) issued its first-ever directive to one of the gas pipeline cartel firms (Enterprise Products Partners LP), to reverse its flow-to-the-ports shipments of gas and propane, and instead make shipments south-to-north, to bring in emergency gas supplies to the North-Central States. This came about amidst the crisis this Winter, when propane users, including farms, households, schools, and institutions, were devastated.

II. Southwest States Crisis

The California, Texas, and Western drought is a national and world-scale water and food emergency. Nevertheless, hydraulic fracturing is consuming critical volumes of water for oil and gas extraction, in areas desperately short of water.

A report released this year by the Boston-based research group Ceres,[1] documented this, by overlaying a map of water-stress regions (from the World Resources Institute), onto the sites of new fracking wells, for the 29-month period January 2011 to May 2013. The results:

• Nearly half (47%) of oil and gas wells opened by fracking in the United States and Canada are in areas of high water stress. In California, New Mexico, and Wyoming, the majority of wells have been drilled in regions of extreme water scarcity. Texes leads all states in the number of such wells, with over 9,000 opened in extremely water-short areas, and another 9,000 in dry-prone locations.

• Only about 5% of all fracking water in these areas has been recycled; that is, 95% is "consumed" and gone. This has directly led, in such places as west Texas and eastern New Mexico, to ranches shutting down, and towns running out of water.

• Over the 29-month study period, fracking consumed 97 billion gallons of water; that is about 45 billion gal/year (0.14 MAFY).

III. National Food Supply Crisis

The states west of the Mississippi River account for majority percentages of U.S. food production—from the grainbelt in the High Plains, to cattle in Texas, to the "fruit-and-vegetable bowl" of California. California alone accounts for over 40% of all the U.S. production of fresh fruits and vegetables, and 20% of milk. All of this is now drastically threatened, by the combination of drought, and the fracking policy directly using water, and creating the oil-and-gas "boom" now disrupting agriculture transportation and the food chain on a vast scale.

The already rising U.S. food prices are set to soar. One example makes the point: beef. The average retail price for beef in March was $5.36 a pound, up more than 33 cents just since December 2013. The U.S. cattle inventory fell to a 63-year low as of January, while cartel exports continue to rise. In Texas, the leading cattle state, where a multi-year drought has caused a severe contraction in cattle numbers, there are the most fracking oil and gas wells in the nation.

---

1. Monika Freyman, "Hydraulic Fracturing & Water Stress: Water Demand by the Numbers," Ceres, February 2014.

IV. Transportation Disaster

Shipments of oil and coal now account for 48% of all rail cargo transported in the United States, mostly due to the spectacular rise in fracked oil production. Oil shipments grew from 9,344 carloads in 2008, to 434,032 in 2013! In 2009, North Dakota produced 200,000 barrels of oil a day; today, it is about 1.1 million a day. Oil shipments increased 5.6% in 2013 over 2012, and 6.6% in 2014 to date over 2013. Besides oil itself, some 40 railcars of sand and other inputs are needed per well fracked.

This oil-ascendence has occurred, as the total rail shipment volume in general had been falling in recent years, as the economy contracts. Total shipments in 2013 were 14.377 million carloads, compared with 14.960 million carloads in 2008. However, no "spare" rail capacity has been freed up in this contraction process to handle the fracking boom. Shipments of other goods are being dramatically displaced, and passenger service too.

In January 2014, the National Association of Railroad Passengers appealed to Transportation Secretary Anthony Foxx, saying that oil transport was disrupting Amtrak service. Amtrak's Empire Builder train (Chicago to Portland, Ore., thence to Seattle), which runs on a BNSF route, has had frequent disruptions in service from Chicago to the West Coast, directly because of BNSF oil shipments from the Bakken Shale oil field. Association president Ross Capon called the situation intolerable: "Crude oil is being given priority over people."

Spectacular accidents, spills, and fires are occurring on the oil trains. On Dec. 30, 2013, a BNSF oil train derailed and exploded near Casselton, N.D., carrying the "tight light crude." Other derailments, explosions, and fires have occurred in Quebec, Alabama, western Pennsylvania, and elsewhere.

But a frenzy of fracking-boom corporate positioning and expansion plans of all kinds is underway—rail, refineries, pipeline connections. The same day as the Casselton disaster, Buffett (Berkshire Hathaway) bought a major interest in Phillips Specialty Products, Inc., a subsidiary of ConocoPhillips, which specializes in pipeline flow-maximization and pipeline-refinery interface technologies. This company is actually a subsidiary of Phillips 66, in which Berkshire Hathaway already owned 27 million shares or about $1 billion—5% ownership; to go with $3 billion in ExxonMobil and $500 million in Suncor.

In January 2013, Phillips 66 bought 2,000 oil railcars through BNSF. It has been using them to run Bakken oil to the East Coast (New Jersey refineries) and will go in the future, to the West Coast. Tesoro Oil bought 1,000 oil railcars for BNSF to move its Bakken oil to its refineries on the West Coast. It is cheaper than either Brent crude or Alaska North Slope oil. This company (Valero) also intends to bring Bakken oil to Vancouver refineries and then ship refined products to Alaska. All this multiplies the dangers.

This is the energy policy Barack Obama has pushed by "phone and pen" (Executive Order) and by encouraging legislation to remove effective regulation of fracking. Fracking oil is the most profitable cargo of Buffett's BNSF Railroad and pipeline network. Is this also involved in Obama's postponements of Keystone pipeline?

V. Policy of Resource Depletion

Measured by the principle of applying increasing advances of science and technology as the determinant of the mode of power in an economy, the reversion to fracking and expansion of retrograde oil and gas for baseline electricity generation and transport is a doomsday policy. We should have never stopped "going nuclear," and must resume going nuclear on a crash basis now. The drive for fusion power is the centerpiece.

Just the factor of diminishing returns of the ever-more-demanding efforts to dig in the Earth's crust for oil and gas, manifests the stupidity. Fracking means resource depletion, and extinction. Nuclear power means the ability *to create natural resources* and, thus, the future.

Unless fracking is stopped, we are on the road to extinction. Right now, the United States accounts for more than 10% of all world crude oil output, which share is accounted for significantly by Texas and North Dakota, and by hydraulic fracturing of tight rock formations. According to the Energy Information Agency March 26 release, the breakdown of the 10% is: over 4% from "tight oil" (fracking), and the remainder from conventional drilling. The foremost oil regions are the Texas Eagle Ford formation and the Bakken formation centered in North Dakota.

The fracking machine is now poised to roll over Mexico, change laws and the Constitution, to cause devastation in the Burgos Basin and elsewhere.

The so-called "fracking revolution" was concocted from the beginning by the commodities wing of Anglo-Dutch imperial finance—the nexus of Royal Dutch Shell, BP, and others—as a matter of energy control, prevention of nuclear power, and destruction of nations.

Look at the role of Dick Cheney. His company, Halliburton, was instrumental in deploying new techniques for the process, and exploiting the protection from regulation, which was arranged by Cheney et al. in the G.W. Bush Administration.

After his stint at Halliburton, Cheney moved on to run the White House. One of his first projects was heading the Energy Task Force (January to June 2001) to devise a national energy strategy—a task force which involved various Cabinet departments meeting with top energy cartel members including Enron, ExxonMobil, Conoco, BP, and Royal Dutch Shell.

In addition to mapping out the areas of Iraqi oil of interest to Anglo-American interests, the task force identified fracking as "one of the fastest growing sources of oil production." It also declared that we should reconsider any regulatory restrictions that do not take "technological advances" into account.

The next step came with the Energy Policy Act of 2005, which amended the Safe Drinking Water Act to exclude fracking from special EPA oversight and specified that the chemicals used in the process were not to be labeled as pollutants under the Clean Water Act! Not surprisingly, this was called the "Halliburton loophole," because of the heavy role played by Halliburton in ensuring that Congress exempted this technology from (rational) environmental oversight.

When Obama came in, in 2009, beholden to the same British financial interests, he simply continued the job.

VI. Sack Warren Buffett

Buffett's activities to cause harm to the nation, through his empire in rail, gas pipelines, Mid-America Energy, and other basic infrastructure operations (as well as insurance, etc.)—maximizing the harm from fracking, are sufficient and urgent grounds to put him out of corporate office. His activities reflect his pedigree as a functionary for the City of London/Wall Street neo-British Empire. He has made a string of strategic acqusitions, which he has deployed to subvert the nation. He works in league with the interlock of Royal Dutch Shell, Chevron, BP, Halliburton, et al., imposing all aspects of the oil and gas "fracking revolution" worldwide. In particular, Buffett was in on vetting Obama for his role as a White House patsy for London.

The BNSF RR was acquired by Buffett's Berkshire

Fortune MPW/Asa Mathat

Warren Buffet has a lock on rail transport in the Midwest, where railcars are unavailable to farmers because they've been diverted to transport gas and oil from fracking.

Hathaway in late 2009, for $34 billion, the largest purchase in Buffett's infamous history. BNSF today operates on 32,500 route miles of track in 28 states, and two provinces in Canada, and dominates outright major regions of the United States.

When, from 2012 to 2013, there was a year-on-year increase in overall U.S. rail cargo volume, fully half of it was accounted for by one company, Buffett's Burlington Northern. In February, BNSF announced it will spend $5 billion this year, with $2.3 billion on its "core network and related assets," including to haul more oil out of the Bakken oil field in North Dakota and Montana.

Buffett is also a foremost gas pipeline owner, getting in on this part of vital U.S. infrastructure during the years of energy deregulation, under Cheney's Energy Task Force perspective. Buffett also has an electricity company, Mid-America, in the Central States; he cancelled plans in 2013 for the company to build a new nuclear power plant in Iowa, and is expanding wind turbine farms.

Buffett ranks among the 85 richest people[2] on Earth, whose combined personal fortunes (over $1.7 trillion) exceed the wealth of the world's poorest 3.5 billion people. His own financial worth is estimated at $53.5 billion, putting him among some 31 Americans on the international list.

In May 2009, Buffett was among those at the Billionaires' Club meeting in New York City with Bill

---

2. OxFam calculations, January 2014.

Gates, George Soros, Ted Turner, Michael Bloomberg, and others, to confer on their goal of population reduction.

In this context, Buffett has played Barack Obama all the way to the present day. In December 2004, Obama, then Senator-elect from Illinois, had a hush-hush session with Buffett, conniving on Obama's new, British-fostered Congressional career. Obama went by chartered jet to Omaha, for a private lunch with Buffett and his daughter Susan Buffett. Obama's Chicago campaign circle tried to keep this secret, given Obama's "man-of-the-people," anti-rich-guy rhetoric. (Reporter Lynn Sweet exposed it at the time.)

In August 2007, Buffett hosted an Omaha fundraiser for Obama, his wife, and children; and another in the Fall.

VII. Congress: Act, or Be Impeached

Every aspect of the so-called fracking boom shows it to be a crime against humanity. But in Wall Street/City of London terms, Obama and cohort Republicans and Democrats represent it as a great achievement, even as the immediate crises worsen of water, food, shipping, heating and means to life.

A few Congressmen, who back the "shale revolution," are calling for small "reforms" to help make the evil system "work better." Sen. John Hoeven (R-N.D.) and Dick Durbin (D-Ill.) are calling for a Federal fund to deter oil rail wrecks. On April 4, Sen. Al Franken (D-Minn.) sent out a letter calling for Congress to set up a new agency—a Safe Transportation of Energy Products Fund, to deal with transporting crude oil. Some 800,000 barrels a day go by tank car out of the Bakken. But you can't tweak evil, to make it better.

On March 25, Senate Energy Committee Chairman Mary Landrieu (D-La.) held a hearing to call for more fracking, and LNG (liquefied natural gas) exports, in order for the U.S. to become the new "superpower" of oil and gas. This was echoed by Ranking Minority Leader Sen. Lisa Murkowski (R-Ak.), and others.

On April 4, the House Natural Resources Committee held a hearing to push fracking in the Monterey Shale formation of California. The pretense was shown in the title, "Energy Independence: Domestic Opportunities to Reverse California's Growing Dependence on Foreign Oil." Chairman Doug Lamborn (R-Colo.) demanded that regulations be lessened, to speed up drilling.

Will Google Take Over the NSA?

by Les Swift

April 17—Google is buying another drone company to add to its collection of robots and drones, and is working on a contact-lens version of Google Glass. At the same time, there are rumors of an even bigger acquisition. According to sources, their sources, and their sources' sources—all known to be as reliable as most sources generally are—Google is preparing an offer to buy the NSA.

"The NSA's stock is way down due to the Snowden scandal," a Wall Street banker/spook told someone in our chain of sources. "Buying it now would be a smart move, and the government might even throw in some other agencies for free."

While Silicon Valley generally supports the move, some are leery of having Google take over the NSA.

"We want it for ourselves," said a top-level source at Facebook, who must remain anonymous because he is actually an agent of a spook agency working as a liaison between his agency and Facebook. "Facebook is the world's largest social network, and would be a perfect fit. We envision turning Facebook into the interface between netizens and the government, with all the business conducted over our network. Taking a page from Obamacare, we could require all U.S. netizens to join Facebook and keep their profiles updated. This would be an evolutionary step in governance, paving the way for true public/private cooperation."

Not everyone is enthusiastic about the prospect, and privacy groups are raising questions.

"While such a deal clearly has potential, we must make sure that if the NSA is privatized, it is done in a way that corrects some of the abuses," said a spokesman for the Society To Regulate the Panopticon. "If done properly, it could be a useful reform.

The Electronic Liberation Front is more skeptical. "We oppose letting Google or Facebook purchase the NSA, as it would give them too much market power," a spokesman for the ELF told us. "We would prefer to see a consortium of stakeholders—the search engines, the social-media sites, the cell-phone outfits, the cable companies, the phone companies, the government contractors, and the advertisers—to give it a broader base and reduce the potential for abuse."

What About the Constitution?

Wall Street supports the move.

"Not only would this give a boost to the stock market, but it would serve to reduce the costs of surveillance," said a senior Wall Street figure who has served in numerous high-level capacities within the U.S. government and supranational agencies. "There is significant overlap between the private-sector surveillance and the government's surveillance, and combining them could streamline the process and cut out the waste. It's a win-win."

"Imagine having access to the NSA network for High Frequency Trading!" exclaimed an executive at a top HFT hedge fund. "That's like a license to print money."

Still, some worry that the move might violate certain ancient texts.

"Get over it," said a top Silicon Valley spokesman. "We don't run the country according to the Dead Sea Scrolls, and no longer should we run it by the Constitution. Both were fine in their day, but their world is gone. It is time to move into the future."

lesswift322@yahoo.com

EIRAmerican System

THE FRIDAY, APRIL 18 MESSAGE!

Start with Our U.S. Economy

by Lyndon H. LaRouche, Jr.

April 18, 2014

If the United States were suddenly freed from the grip of the present Barack Obama Administration, there would be the immediate possibility of both halting the presently growing threat of a global thermonuclear war now building up. This could not be a reasonable possibility unless the United States of America, itself, were freed from the grip of the present economic policies of that Obama administration. An appropriately immediate change in U.S.A. domestic economic policy would be an adequate foundation for an immediate change to that net effect, not only within the U.S.A., but also globally.

The essentials of that change in U.S.A. economic policy are, therefore, now presented here, as follows for presentation on this present date. The implications are, immediately global, economic and globally strategic in their implications: as follows.

A succinct, but indispensable report of the facts, is:

The U.S.A. Economic Reform!

The post-1492 A.D. foundations of a new republic in North America had been lain with the founding and development of the Massachusetts Bay Colony under the leadership of the Winthrops and Mathers; the economic and related advances made by that colony had supplied a leading edge of economic and cultural development for the colony, and also for related improvements in the political and economic systems in Europe. However, the Dutch imperialists had crushed that Colony, which was later rebuilt, at the personal prompting of Cotton Mather and the genius of the Benjamin Franklin who had been mustered to a role of leadership in politics, economics, and science under the rising leadership of Franklin within both North America and in influence within Europe. The founding of the United States, despite the evil practices of the British Empire, then, as now, had repeatedly inspired European nations, and others, to regain the rights which founding principles of the United States had stipulated, and otherwise implied.

The foundations of that United States, under Benjamin Franklin, and General-and-President George Washington, were lain under the economics genius of the Franklin successor, and original founder of the economic policy of the American system of political economy, under Treasury Secretary Alexander Hamilton.

Secretary (and General officer) Hamilton, had inspired related progress in the effort to free Europe from the evil grip of the rising British imperial tyranny which dominates Europe's nations to the present day. Worse, with the British ouster of Germany's Chancellor Bismarck, that same British empire and its Dutch accomplices, had set into motion a pattern of virtually perpetual warfare and imperial tyranny throughout most of the world as a whole, up through the present day of warfare in Europe and beyond, up through the present moment.

The following facts of history must be taken into account:

With the death of the Benjamin Franklin who had, in effect, led the process of creation of the then future United States, the leading intellectual authority for the policies of the young United States had been, chiefly, the original Secretary of the Treasury of the United States, Alexander Hamilton, one of the world's most accomplished geniuses in the matters of economic policy which the trans-Atlantic nations have actually experienced. Hamilton's policies, had been revived and continued by Secretary of State and, later, President of the United States, John Quincy Adams.

However, British agents, such as the professional British assassin Aaron Burr, had financed a takeover of the Presidency of the United States under British-owned scoundrels such as Andrew Jackson and Martin Van Buren. That latter pair had controlled the Presidency of the United States under the direction of British imperial banking interests operating through implicitly treasonous circles associated with Wall Street financial corruption of the United States' institutions, then, as now.

Later, a close follower of John Quincy Adams, President Abraham Lincoln, had rescued the United States from a succession of British agents led by the British Empire's leading agent and spy, Aaron Burr, who had seized control over the United States, once again, through buying up treasonous Presidents such as Andrew Jackson and Martin Van Buren. Similarly, the United States once victorious against the British Empire's attempted seizure of power over the United States, was shattered by the British-directed and financed assassination of President Abraham Lincoln: and so matters have gone repeatedly, excepting under a relative handful of worthy U.S. Presidents who were not either fools or outrightly agents of the British Empire and its interests.

Since then, we have enjoyed a number of truly honorable, even great Presidents of the United States, but with the successful assassination of a great President, William McKinley, and McKinley's replacement by a British-trained agent, Theodore Roosevelt, and scoundrels and virtual traitors such as Woodrow Wilson, Calvin Coolidge, and Herbert Hoover, only the election of President Franklin D. Roosevelt, saved the United States, and the world at large from a virtual state of Hell into which the election of Harry S Truman sold the virtual soul of the United States, despite the devotion of President Dwight D. Eisenhower and the soon martyred John F. Kennedy. Since the assassination of President Kennedy, despite the personal role of Presidents Ronald Reagan and William Clinton, the United States had been send down the road toward Hell under such as the scions of the Bush, Cheney, and Obama breeds.

What, then, is our excuse for the United States' own frequent departure from the genius represented by Benjamin Franklin, President George Washington, and Treasury Secretary Hamilton. Simply, Hamilton was assassinated by a paid British assassin, Aaron Burr (who had funded the Andrew Jackson and Martin Van Buren Presidencies' establishment). However, that could not have happened but for the earlier corruption expressed by Presidents John Adams, Thomas Jefferson, and James Madison. There had been two excellent Presidents, James Monroe and John Quincy Adams, but since the ouster of John Quincy Adams from the Presidency, the honest Presidents had been quickly assassinated; this had continued, until the Presidency of Abraham Lincoln, who was, himself, assassinated by the actions and agents of the British Empire, itself.

The crucial fact is, that most of the Presidents of the United States were in opposition to the Federal Constitution of the United States, and betrayed the vital interest of the United States for the sake of local interests within the states, for which the State of New York (especially the British and other Manhattan banks there) was a leading feature, i.e., Wall Street, then, as now.

What, then, has been the root of the chronic British corruption of the Presidency of the United States this far? The answer to that question is properly to be located in the fact and implications of the assassination of Secretary of the Treasury Alexander Hamilton, by the professional British assassin, Aaron Burr. Assassinations aside, the name of the general body of the implicitly treasonous corruption, was "sectionalism:" the division of the states of the United States according to local interests, in spite of essentially contrary national interests. The name of that corruption was "states' rights." The issue was clearly defined during Alexander Hamilton's tenure as Secretary of the Treasury.

Now, our United States is in the throes of a general economic breakdown-crisis, a crisis which must be recognized as, largely a product of the British imperial control over the United States which has been largely dependent upon the British monetarist interests' control over the U.S.A.'s own "Wall Street" management.

The following remarks presented here, by me go di-

This memorial stone was placed where "the patriot, soldier, statesman, and jurist Alexander Hamilton" was felled by assassin Aaron Burr. The root of the chronic British corruption of the Presidency of the United States, LaRouche writes, is properly to be located in the fact and implications of the assassination of Hamilton, by Burr.

rectly to the core of the presently mortal threats to both a general peace among nations, and to the threats of the virtual extinction of the United States itself.

Alexander Hamilton Now

From the time of Alexander Hamilton's assassination by the British spy and assassination agent Aaron Burr, the United States had lost an entire aspect of its national sovereignty, until the fortunate advent of the Presidencies of James Monroe and John Quincy Adams. With the fresh takeover of the U.S. Presidency through the role of the financial backing of the British agents Andrew Jackson and Martin Van Buren, the United States had, *de facto*, lost its actual sovereignty, through the elections of witting British agents in the Presidency, or by the assassinations of those suspected of patriotism, until the election of President Abraham Lincoln.

With Lincoln's assassination by, explicitly, the named agents of the British empire, the U.S. Presidencies vacillated with shifts from some heroes, such as Grant and Garfield and, then, to opportunists or worse. The last truly great President, prior to President Franklin D. Roosevelt, had been the assassinated hero William McKinley. Apart from the President Harding who died of poisoning (allegedly from eating oysters) during a railway crossing of the Great American Desert, only one decent President served until President Franklin D. Roosevelt, after the assassination of President William McKinley. After Presidents Franklin D. Roosevelt, Dwight Eisenhower, and the assassinated John F. Kennedy, no decent presidents served until Presidents Ronald Reagan and William Clinton, and none since. Thus, in the main, throughout the history of the United States, the Presidency has been dominated by the effect of fewer honest Presidents than British-promoted scoundrels.[1]

The difference has lain with the factor of corruption rooted in the practice of "states' rights," as through the mechanisms of the elements of the U.S. Congress identified with the members of the Senate and House of Representatives: often the Senate, as is notable from the cases of the pro-slavery states, and related kinds of influences.

The most notable feature of the states' rights feature of the U.S. political system, has been centered (to a relatively lesser degree) in New England, but chiefly in Britain-dominated Wall Street connections. The concentration of relatively great financial wealth in the channels of British-influenced U.S. financial affairs, has remained the chief route of moral and other political corruption of the United States since the assassination of the Alexander Hamilton, who, following the demise of Benjamin Franklin, had been the efficient constitutional voice of the economic principles of the United States.

On the better side of the news, on this account,

---

1. In general, assassinated U.S. Presidents were usually heroes of our republic, and had been selected for such treatment, for precisely that reason: including President John F. Kennedy, his brother virtually nominated for President, and President Ronald Reagan, who survived the attack.

whenever the United States enjoyed the benefit of a government dominated by the Hamilton tradition, as under John Quincy Adams, Abraham Lincoln, or similarly inclined Presidents, the United States has tended to be its own true self; under other conditions, the results tended to be implicitly Wall Street influences. So, international money-flows have dominated the economy and, to a great degree, the policy-making of the U.S. Federal and also state governments.

Alexander Hamilton's Genius

However:

Once Hamilton's four official principles of economy were actually put in place, now, the United States could, now, quickly regain its originally intended constitutional principle, that done through the belated four great principles of the U.S. Federal Constitution set forth by Treasury Secretary Hamilton under his term in office.

Hamilton's measures installed while Secretary of the Treasury, are four in total. Three of these are customarily referenced by relevant scholars of our Federal Constitution: (1) "Report on Public Credit;" (2) "Report on A National Bank;" (4) "On the Subject of Manufactures." The most crucial, for the defense of our national system of government, was, however, the third, (3) "Opinion on the Constitutionality of a National Bank." It was the latter, the "Opinion on the Constitutionality of a National Bank" which prompted British agent Aaron Burr's assassination of Alexander Hamilton: over the so-called "states right" exception to the Federal Constitution. Every evil of our national practice since the passage of the Constitution, has been a result of the treasonous "states' right" dogma of interpretation, as by President John Adams, Thomas Jefferson, James Madison, and the enemy, Aaron Burr's puppets, Andrew Jackson and Martin Van Buren, in particular. The defects of the Presidency, including the selection of bad Presidents, have been premised, essentially on the inherent violation of the Federal Constitution accomplished through the pitting of the authority of the individual States of the United States, against the Federal Constitution itself. The directly British-directed assassination of President Abraham Lincoln, is an outstanding case, as was the assassination of President William McKinley in favor of the Confederacy-trained President Theodore Roosevelt, a typical case, as was the case of the evil Woodrow Wilson, and of Presidents Calvin Coolidge, Herbert Hoover, and Harry S Truman. Presidents George Bush, George W. Bush, Jr., and Barack Obama are of the same treasonous genre-in-fact.

Time To Make Things Right, at Last

The time has long passed, when we could have made right the evil injustices which sundry enemies of our United States, from without, or within, have left behind them. Our only recourse available now, is to fix, for the future, what ever have been wrong in the past. The practical task before us, presently, is: how might we, nonetheless, do something now, to remedy the hurts and atrocities from the past, even with respect to the already deceased? What moral principle meets the challenge of a shameful past?

On that account, we must consider, first of all, what justice, in the name of repair, might be afforded to those who have been cruelly injured by bad law, especially those who have lost the stuffing to defend themselves against presently continuing injustices, persons who have lost the will to fight for their own rights, or those of their fellow-citizens?

The only sufficient reply to such questions as that, is: How do we make right, what had otherwise been going wrong? How can we nourish our cheated fellow-citizens, adults, but, most urgently the saving of the minds and morals of the under-aged? How can we bring justice, where there has been injustice? How might we bring those who have seen injustice, to see real justice born again? How does one right what Hitler and also the British empire did against the Jews who suffered under Hitler and his like still today?

There is an actual remedy for such errors of the past. The answer lies in the nature of the purpose of mankind's having existed as a species of its specific nature: the progress of the human species from the failures of the past, to the immortality of the future mankind which actually progresses.

We are, usually, sadly mistaken, by attributing the meaning of human life to what has been experienced in human life lived so far, when, in fact, the meaning of the individual human life is expressed in the consequences of a human life already lived. That is to say, the future outcome of that life which had been lived. It is precisely that distinction of human life which distinguishes mankind from the beasts. The objective to be served is the increase of the productive powers of future labor achieved through those creative actions which enable the future society to realize the gains of future humanity which the earlier society could not have achieved: the specifically creative powers unique to the progressively higher achievement of future mankind, than the past generations.

The only true purpose of the present life, is to create a future mankind of greater powers for achievement, in principle, relative to the relative failures buried in the past. That is the only true measure of any person's, or any society's meaningful existence as a worthy member of the human species.

The Explanation:

That is the true principle of the human species, which distinguishes the human being from all of the beasts.

The standard for performance of the member of the human species, is to increase the relative energy-flux density of performance per capita and unit of passage of time of one generation to the next successor. If mankind fails to evolve into the equivalent, in performance, from a less productive generation to a more productive one, that society tends to have failed in meeting its required achievements. Thus, neglect the increase of the energy-flux density of the human individual's typical performance, from less productive, to more productive in terms of energy-flux density (to greater power for productivity), and society would have failed to meet the moral standard of the human species. The "green" doctrine is, therefore, to be damned as being intrinsically evil.

Indeed, the trend downward of mankind's progress since the beginning of the Twentieth Century, reflects a moral degeneration of the relevant sections of the human population in the relevant region of the human society as a whole, a relative unfitness to lead society's policy-shaping, and the degeneration of that sector of mankind relative to the others.

Thus, the British Queen is clearly to be defined as intrinsically evil, as, similarly, those sections of American and European society whose characteristic is to resist an efficient increase of the energy-flux density of mankind generally, which is to say a "beastly" section of the human species in the large.

A.) Glass Steagall.
B.) National Banking/Dept. of Treasury.
C.) National Credit System.
D.) Science-Driver Program.

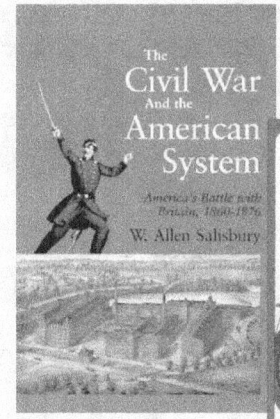

LaRouche: Empire's War Drive Stalemated, But Threat Remains

by The Editors

April 21—The British Empire's demented drive for global thermonuclear war, most recently using the Ukraine theater as a fulcrum, has been stymied over the past week, Lyndon LaRouche commented in discussions with associates on April 19. But the stalemate emerging from the April 17 quadripartite Geneva agreement, is highly unstable. The British Empire's war drive will either be derailed by removing President Obama from office, or it will again escalate rapidly towards thermonuclear confrontation, this time with direct involvement of the British Empire.

"The entire operation so far, is now stalemated," LaRouche stated. "Which means the next stage is: the British Empire moves in. Which means, Australia, and points in the Middle East, and trying to pull the United States in. But if they can't pull the United States in, it ain't going to work! Without the United States, they cannot start a Eurasian war.

"So it's an interesting situation. That's the stalemate. The British are not in a situation to declare war, unless they can get the United States to push it through, and there are blocks right now."

LaRouche then took note of the pressure Obama is coming under as the result of a Florida judge's decision to compel the FBI to release 92,000 pages of documents relevant to Saudi financing of activities related to 9/11; and he underscored the strategic significance of the Kesha Rogers campaign for the Senate from Texas, which can blow open the entire situation in the Democratic Party nationally, to good effect.

The Neo-Nazi Factor

The crucial issue which Russian President Vladimir Putin has used to gum up the works on the war drive for the moment, LaRouche explained, is that the neo-Nazi squadristi—which the British and Obama intentionally put in the driver's seat in their illegitimate and unelected Ukrainian government—must be disarmed and demobilized, as part of the Geneva agreement. "Putin put something in very clearly, on the question of the conditions, in terms of Ukraine," LaRouche said. "That there has to be no thuggery continued in Ukraine. That's where the block is. And Putin says, there's no giving in on that, that these guys have to surrender their guns."

Indeed, when Right Sector squadristi attacked pro-Russian protesters in eastern Ukraine on Easter Sunday morning, killing a reported four people in a firefight, the Western media broke its usual black propaganda profile, and accurately reported the Right Sector's effort to blow up the Geneva deal.

Meanwhile, the eastward expansion of NATO to Russia's borders continues, with reports of the possible forward-basing of some 10,000 American troops in Poland, and similar deployments. In his four-hour April 17 video town hall meeting, President Putin denounced the eastward expansion of NATO—which is occurring despite early 1990s promises from the first Bush Administration that this would not happen—and commented: "If we don't do anything, Ukraine will be drawn into NATO sometime in the future. We'll be told 'This doesn't concern you,' and NATO ships will dock

State Department

The April 17 meeting in Geneva (shown here), in which the U.S., EU, Ukraine, and Russia participated, stymied the British war drive, but the situation remains fragile, LaRouche stated, as long as Obama remains in office. The photo shows Russian Foreign Minister Lavrov (left foreground), U.S. Secretary of State Kerry (oppposite, second from left); and Ukrainian Foreign Minister Deshchytsia (across the table).

in Sevastopol [in Crimea], the city of Russia's naval glory."

Putin also warned: "Let me remind you that the Federation Council of Russia [the upper house of parliament] gave the President the right to use the Armed Forces in Ukraine. I very much hope that I will not have to exercise this right and that, through political and diplomatic means, we will be able to resolve all the pressing, if not to say burning, issues in Ukraine."

Those remarks of Putin's have been widely covered in the West. But what has been almost totally blacked out are his comments at the same meeting, warning that the U.S.-NATO ballistic missile defense system is even more threatening to Russia than NATO's eastward expansion.

"I'll use this opportunity to say a few words about our talks on missile defense," Putin said. "This issue has no less, and probably even more importance, than NATO's eastward expansion.... At the expert level, everyone understands very well that, if these systems are deployed closer to our borders, our ground-based strategic missiles will be within their striking range.... If they deploy these elements in Europe, we'll have to do something in response, as we've said so many times.... We'll do everything to guarantee the security of the Russian people, and I'm sure we'll succeed."

LaRouche took note of these developments, and concluded his discussion with associates by saying: "This is what goes on the record as of now, as spoken, here, at this point. That defines what we're saying is the issue of war, as of now. We now recognize, we are a factor in this process. And what I'm doing is a factor in this process of determining peace and war issues."

Further Breaks on War Avoidance

With the opportunity to push back against the British Empire war drive provided by the Geneva agreements of April 17, some voices in U.S. institutions have decided to press the point. On April 19, Reuters published a lengthy special report, detailing how the Bush and Obama Administrations wrecked the prospects of strategic collaboration with Russia. The report revolved around comments by an unnamed senior Obama Administration official, who bluntly stated that it was Washington, not Moscow that blew up the potential for strategic partnership—even after Putin was the first foreign leader to offer and deliver strong support to the United States following the 9/11 attacks. Under the dominant influence of Vice President Dick Cheney, President George W. Bush responded to the Russian cooperation by abrogating the Anti-Ballistic Missle (ABM) Treaty, to deploy the very missile defense shield into the European theater that remains the number one source of potential thermonuclear war.

In November 2002, the Bush Administration escalated the confrontation with Russia by pressing for seven former Warsaw Pact nations and former Soviet republics to be invited to join NATO by 2004. President Obama further exacerbated the conflict by moving forward with the ABM deployments, and by attempting to bypass Putin during the period when Putin ally Dmitri Medvedev was Russian President.

In addition to the unnamed senior Administration

official, the Reuters report quoted several former U.S. ambassadors to the Soviet Union, and then Russia, who are still active, including Jack Matlock and James Collins, and former Bush National Security Council Director for Russia Thomas Graham. Graham, in particular, argued that the United States had missed a golden opportunity with the fall of the Soviet Union, to abolish NATO and create a new tripartite security structure for Europe involving the United States, a reunified Europe, and Russia.

The Hair-Trigger Remains

The Easter ambush near the eastern Ukrainian city of Slavyansk highlights the fragility of the situation on the ground. A statement by the Russian Foreign Ministry following the attack stated, "The Russian side is indignant at this provocation of the militants, which proves Kiev's authorities are not willing to control and disarm the nationalists and extremists."

As LaRouche warned in his April 19 dialogue with colleagues, it is critical to watch carefully for British-engineered provocations to draw the United States deeper into direct confrontation with Russia.

The *Economist*, a leading voice of the British Crown and the City of London, called for just such a provocation this week, editorializing: "The West needs to show Mr Putin that further action will be costly. So far, its rhetoric has marched far ahead of its willingness to act—only adding to the aura of weakness. Not enough is at stake in Ukraine to risk war with a nuclear-armed Russia. And European voters will not put up with gas shortages, so an embargo is not plausible. But the West has other cards to play. One is military. NATO should announce that it will hold exercises in central and eastern Europe, strengthen air and cyber defences there and immediately send some troops, missiles and aircraft to the Baltics and Poland. NATO members should pledge to increase military spending.

"Another card is sanctions, so far imposed on only a few people close to Mr Putin. It is time for a broad visa ban on powerful Russians and their families. France should cancel the sale of warships to Russia. A more devastating punishment would be to cut Russia off from dollars, euros and sterling. Such financial sanctions, like those that led Iran to negotiate over its nuclear programme, would deprive Russia of revenues from oil and gas exports, priced in dollars, and force it to draw on reserves to pay for most of its imports. They would be costly to the West, especially the City of London, but worth it. Impose them now, and give Mr Putin reason to pause. Do any less and the price next time will be even higher."

Ambrose Evans-Pritchard, the London *Telegraph* voice for the British intelligence establishment, has written several recent columns, reporting that the Obama Administration has already launched covert financial warfare against Russia, cutting off access to credit lines and forcing the Russian government to dip deep into its financial stability reserve funds to roll over debts amounting to more than $10 billion per month.

Other Fronts for Provocation

This week, Vice President Joe Biden is in Kiev conferring with Ukrainian government officials, while President Obama travels to Asia to meet with treaty allies Japan, South Korea, and the Philippines (he is also visiting Malaysia). The absence of a China stopover is indicative of the fact that relations between Washington and Beijing are more strained than they have been in years, largely due to Obama's "Asia pivot"—the policy of promoting a doctrine of Air-Sea Battle that blurs the lines between conventional and nuclear war. Chinese officials will be closely watching for indications that Obama is looking to tighten the containment of China through deeper military arrangements with the three allied countries of the East and South China sea regions.

London has also been aggressively promoting the idea that a new North Korean crisis could erupt at any moment. An exclusive story published in the *Telegraph* earlier this month warned that a new purge is underway in Pyongyang, citing a recent North Korean intelligence defector called "Mr. K" who has provided a stream of inside intelligence on the splits in the North Korean leadership.

Between the Obama trip to the Far East and the uncertainty about the situation inside North Korea, the Asia-Pacific region could also detonate into crisis at any moment.

It is precisely in this context that LaRouche has continued to warn that the danger of conflict is not centered in Ukraine, but is global in nature—and is driven by the growing desperation in London and Wall Street that the current financial system is doomed and a "little war" could be the best vehicle for settling financial accounts without diminishing the power of the Empire over global affairs.

Documentation

Ukrainian Parties Warn Of Civil War, WWIII

On the eve of the April 17 quadrilateral negotiations in Geneva, 27 leaders of Ukrainian parties and organizations appealed to UN, European, and U.S. officials to promote exclusively "peaceful negotiations" as the pathway to a resolution of conflicts within Ukraine, rather than promoting civil war and risking the detonation of World War III. The statement, published below, charged that the current regime in Kiev was illegally installed and is continuing the neo-Nazi slogans of the Euromaidan insurgency, by which the Feb. 22 coup against Ukraine's elected President was made. Thus, these Ukrainian activists are in total disagreement with the U.S. State Department, whose spokesman on April 18 repeated the view that there was no coup and the current authorities are legitimate.

The citation in the appeal of calls to "shoot 'separatists'" refers to Member of Parliament Iryna Farion of the racist Svoboda Party, which holds three ministerial portfolios and the Prosecutor General's Office in the coup-installed regime; Earlier this month Farion told an interviewer that Kiev should be "much tougher" on anti-coup protesters in eastern Ukraine. "I would have simply have shot them," she said, "Listen, the enemy is ruling on our land.... They should have been driven out of here back in 1654. The measures should be much tougher. Because these creatures who are coming here deserve only one thing: death. (1654 refers to the Treaty of Pereyaslav between Ukrainian Cossack Hetman Bohdan Khmelnytsky and the Russian Tsar Alexander Mikhailovich.)

Natalia Vitrenko, a signer of the appeal, toured Europe in February to expose the ongoing coup in Ukraine.

Many of the signers were also signatories on a Jan. 25 appeal (*EIR*, Jan. 31, 2014) for world action to prevent the coup, which highlighted the neo-Nazi symbols of the Euromaidan, as well as the threat to Ukraine's economy and sovereignty from the Association Agreement with the European Union, the rejection of which by then-President Victor Yanukovych in November 2013 served as the pretext for the regime-change action that was named the Euromaidan. Three of the, signers, Natalia Vitrenko, Volodymyr Marchenko, and Valeri Sergachov, toured Europe in February-March to expose the Western-backed neo-Nazi revival and coup in Ukraine (*EIR*, March 7, 2014).

'Stop the War of the Self-Proclaimed Ukrainian Authorities Against Their Own People!'

To: UN Secretary-General Ban Ki-moon, President of the European Union, Herman Van Rompuy, and President of the Russian Federation Vladimir Putin

We, leaders of Ukrainian political parties and public organizations, urgently request that you take all measures necessary to stop the civil war in Ukraine, defend the civilian population of southeast Ukraine against political repression, humiliation, and physical elimination by illegal bands of ultraradicals, the National Guard that has been set up for punitive actions, and the Armed Forces of Ukraine.

We draw your attention to the fact that yesterday's oppositionists, who proclaimed neo-Nazi slogans like "Ukraine for Ukrainians," "Stab the Muscovites," and "Glory to the nation—death to the enemies!" and held mass torch marches with Nazi insignia and portraits of Nazi collaborators Bandera and Shukhevych, have now become the government, as a result of a coup d'état. And now, as representatives of the government, they are continuing to talk about "the physical destruction of 8 million Russians," shooting "separatists," and so forth, in contradiction to the norms and principles of international law and the Constitution of Ukraine. Acting on a neo-Nazi attitude toward national minorities and the Russian-speaking population, as being ethnic groups that are hostile to the creation of a mono-ethnic state, the Acting President of Ukraine has decided to use the Armed Forces against civilians, violating the ban on this, stated in Article 17 of the Constitution of Ukraine.

We believe that the authorities in Ukraine are committing illegal acts, punishable by law, from the standpoint of the December 9, 1948 Genocide Convention, Article 3. The rights of citizens of Ukraine, guaranteed by the Constitution of Ukraine, the International Pact on Civil and Political Rights, the European Convention on the Defense of Human Rights and Basic Freedoms, the Universal Declaration on Human Rights, and the UN Charter, are being violated. The Russian-speaking population of southeastern Ukraine has been falsely labeled "separatists," thus subverting its right to defend its rights and freedoms, dignity, life, and security against infringement by the neo-Nazis who have seized power.

We are convinced that demands to give the Russian language the status of an official language and to shift Ukraine to a federative form of organization have nothing in common with separatism, but, on the contrary, are mechanisms for preserving Ukraine as a single, democratic state, providing justice and development for the southeastern regions within it.

Instead, a decision has been taken to use the Armed Forces of Ukraine—tanks, artillery, Grad rocket-launchers, airplanes, helicopters, and missiles—to kill the country's people, covering these actions with propaganda lies about "separatism," "terrorism," and "Russian interference."

In reality, the Ukrainian Army has already brought tanks and APCs into the Donbass. There are casualties. This is a war, declared against the country's people.

We condemn it! Peaceful negotiations, consideration of the legitimate demands of the culturally Russian population, and a ban on neo-Nazi parties and movements is the pathway to a democratic resolution of the conflict. The "force" scenario is the pathway to a fratricidal war in Ukraine and the unleashing of a Third World War on the European continent.

We ask your immediate intervention for a solution to the crisis.

Respectfully,

Alexander V. Bondarchuk, Ukrainian Labor Party (Marxist-Leninist), People's Deputy of Ukraine, 2nd, 3rd, 4th sessions of the Supreme Rada; **Natalia M. Vitrenko**, Progressive Socialist Party of Ukraine, Doctor of Economic Sciences, People's Deputy of Ukraine, 2nd and 3rd sessions of Supreme Rada; **Sergei V. Dovgan**, Honorary Chairman of the Peasant Party of Ukraine, People's Deputy of Ukraine, 2nd and 3rd sessions of the Supreme Rada; **Lyudmila P. Kayotkina**, All-Ukraine Women's Public Organization "Gift of Life," Deputy of Donetsk Regional Parliament, 5th session; **Yelena A. Mazur**, All-Ukraine Public Organization "For the Union of Ukraine, Belarus and Russia," People's Deputy of Ukraine, 3rd session of Supreme Rada; **Tatyana A. Makarenko**, "Russkaya Obshchina" (Russian Community), Dnepropetrovsk; **Gennadi V. Makarov**. Coordinating Council of Russian Organizations in Eastern Ukraine, Russkoye Veche; **Volodymyr R. Marchenko**, Ukrainian Federation of Labor, People's Deputy of Ukraine, 1st, 2nd, 3rd sessions of Supreme Rada; **Alexander V. Svistunov**, Russian Movement of Ukraine, Deputy of Supreme Soviet of Autonomous Republic of Crimea, 5th session; **Valeri A. Sergachov**, Kiev Rus Party, Deputy of Odessa Regional Parliament, 5th session; **Valentin B. Lukyanik**, Union of Orthodox Brotherhoods of Ukraine; **Olga N. Solovenko**, Eurasian People's Union, Deputy of Odessa Regional Parliament, 5th session; **Yuri N. Yegorov**, Orthodox Choice; **Pavel V. Tishchenko**, Kharkov regional "Trudovaya Kharkovshchina," People's Deputy of Ukraine, 3rd session; **Viktor V. Silenko**, All-Ukrainian Association of Russian Compatriots; **Nina I. Sorba**, Assembly of Orthodox Women of Ukraine; **Vladlena V. Kalenskaya**, Just Cause; **Vasili F. Kuvshinov**, Union of Soviet Officers, Chigirin; **Vladimir G. Gatkevich**, Veterans of War and Labor of the Smelyansk Electromechanical Plant; **Gennadi A. Snoz**, Rukh Molodi, Cherkassy organization; **Alexander I. Ogorodnikov**, Union of Soviet Officers, Uman; **Viktor M. Parkhomenko**, Registered Cossacks, Chigirin; **Bogdan Y. Kucherenko**, Bastion, historical-patriotic organization, Chigirin; **Vladimir V. Bogatyrev**, Russian Union; **Alexander P. Varushko**, United Slavic Front, Dnepropetrovsk; **Igor Vorobyov**, Russian Union of the Donbass, Lugansk; **Alexander Yeryomenko**, OKO Diamanta charitable foundation, Odessa; **Galina S. Sazonova**, ZOSh Vega Club, Kiev.

'Silk Road Lady' on the Potential For a 21st-Century Peace Order

Helga Zepp-LaRouche was interviewed on the Chinese CCTV program <u>Dialogue</u> in Beijing on Feb. 20, 2014; the half-hour interview first aired on April 14. Dialogue is a prime-time daily English-language talk show, which reaches viewers across China, and more than 80 million subscribers around the world. Yang Rui, who conducted the interview, is one of the most prominent journalists in China, having interviewed numerous foreign ministers and heads of state on his program. For foreign viewers, Dialogue is the preeminent means for following the debate in China; for Chinese viewers, it is the primary venue to hear the opinions of world leaders on questions relating to China. Here is an edited transcript.

Yang Rui: Plans for a New Silk Road for the 21st Century are being promoted by Chinese President Xi Jinping: He imagines an economic belt along the route of the Silk Road traveled more than 2,000 years ago. The proposal has attracted widespread support, as a means of boosting trade and cooperation across the two continents.

One of the keenest supporters is an international thinktank, the Schiller Institute, led by its President, Mrs. Helga Zepp-LaRouche, who first advocated the idea of a Eurasian Land-Bridge more than 20 years ago. She joins us now in the video studio to discuss the importance of a modern Silk Road.

What differences will it make to Central Asia and the world? Will Eurasia emerge as a new economic power, and what impact would it have on China, and the Asia-pacific region?

[A video is then shown, on the Han Dy-nasty Silk Road, as a model for international cooperation.]

Yang: Welcome to Dialogue, Madam.

Helga Zepp-LaRouche: Hello.

Yang: Helga, you have been promoting the idea of constructing a so-called Eurasian Land-Bridge, which is very similar to the brainchild of Mr. Xi Jinping—the Silk Road that goes through the Central Asia region. Now, you're sometimes referred to as the New Silk Road Lady. Is that a title you're proud of?

Zepp-LaRouche: Yes. I don't remember who exactly came up with this idea, but I think it was because I organized hundreds of conferences and seminars in the last 24 years for this concept.

Yang: So, you enjoy the copyright.

Zepp-LaRouche: Well, yes, so to speak.

"I think we have to move away from geopolitics," Zepp-LaRouche said. "Because geopolitics gave the world two world wars in the 20th Century. And if we stay with geopolitics, I think we are on the verge of a Third World War."

Sun Yat-sen's Brainchild

Yang: In 1917, if my memory is correct, Dr. Sun Yat-sen, President of the Republic of China, was the first to follow the idea of building the Eurasian Land-Bridge, hopefully to connect China with Russia, because he put forward the idea of getting united with the Russians, the Soviets, the Communist Party, workers and farmers. What do you think of his brainchild, and have you gotten any inspiration from his proposals?

Zepp-LaRouche: Yes. Because Dr. Sun Yat-sen was obviously very much concerned about the well-being of the population, and he also saw in the railway connection between all these different countries, a way to preserve peace. And that has been exactly what has been inspiring us to go with the Eurasian Land-Bridge, because it was meant, from the beginning, after the collapse of the Soviet Union, as a peace order for the 21st Century.

Yang: So, do you think that the well-being of the people should be the vital problem of China in those days? That's the title of a book written by Dr. Sun Yat-sen [*The Vital Problem of China*, 1917—ed.].

Zepp-LaRouche: Yes. He was very much inspired also by Lincoln, and the idea of government by the people, for the people, and of the people, and therefore I think that that is what we have to think about today too.

Yang: What's the relevance between Abraham Lincoln and the New Silk Road?

Zepp-LaRouche: Well, because it is a system of physical-economy. Nowadays, we are very much in monetarist terms. People think about profit, and that has led the world to its present terrible crisis of a threatened collapse of the financial system. And we have to go back to the idea of physical-economy, which is associated with the industrial revolution of America, which was the result of the policies of Lincoln, who also created a land-bridge across America.

So, we have to go back to the ideas of a system of protectionism, of taking as the only source of wealth

Chinese President Xi Jingping (center) proposed an "economic belt," similar to the concept of the Silk Road, at the Shanghai Cooperation Organization meeting in Kazakhstan. He is shown here at the SCO in September 2013.

the creativity of the people, and not think about buying cheap, selling dear, the idea that's associated with free trade.

So, if the whole world wants to get out of the present crisis, it has to be based on the ideas which already led to industrial revolutions in the past.

Yang: All politics are local. Therefore, trade protectionism, whatever the label you use to describe protectionism—it's domestic politics.

Let's get back to examining the history of the ancient Silk Road. I wonder if you can brief us about how the Silk Road involves much of Asia, and parts of Europe.

Zepp-LaRouche: In the ancient times, or now?

Yang: Ancient times.

Zepp-LaRouche: Well, 2,000 years ago, the ancient Silk Road connected cultures and people, and there were all kinds of modes of traveling: horses, camels, ships; and it did create the basis for a tremendous increase of wealth of all the countries which participated in the Silk Road. So, I think if we revive this conception, it will be to the benefit of all participating countries.

Yang: Central Asia is the bridge linking the European countries with the Asia-Pacific economies. However, do you think the economic belt that President Xi

Jinping raised when he was attending a summit meeting for the Shanghai Cooperation Organization in Kazakhstan would help the region of Central Asia to prosper, and enjoy true prosperity?

Zepp-LaRouche: These countries suffer still from the monoculture [agriculture] of the Soviet Union. Many countries have a lack of water. So when we are talking about the expansion of the Eurasian Land-Bridge, or the New Silk Road, it's not just railways, or means of transport; it is a new economic platform, which transforms the entire economy of the region into a much higher productivity.

It also involves the question of corridors. You know, we have developed the idea that the Silk Road should probably have 100-kilometer width. You put in new energy production and distribution, communications, and this way you make areas which are landlocked, and don't have access to the sea or rivers, investment-friendly, like countries which are on the seaside or on river systems.

It basically means that the landlocked areas of all of Eurasia will enjoy the same benefits as countries on the maritime coasts. And this will lead to a new era of economics. The Land-Bridge, or Silk Road, conception is not just more cooperation among countries. If you think back, evolution of civilization happened first by cultures and countries settled at the coasts; then they would move through the rivers—

Moving Past Geopolitics

Yang: And even through the Opium War, and the slave trade, to begin with, the success story, the early part of the economic success story of the European powers. I hope you can understand that there's a sense of victimhood by many Asians.

Central Asia used to be the backyard of the former Soviet Union. Therefore, do understand the geopolitical concerns of the Russians, when it comes to the future of, say, the New Silk Road, or the economic belt, that threaten to connect China to Central Asia with the developed European part.

Zepp-LaRouche: I think we have to move away from geopolitics. Because geopolitics gave the world two world wars in the 20th Century. And if we stay with geopolitics, I think we are on the verge of a Third World War. And therefore, I think the conception of the Eurasian Land-Bridge, which is a little bit larger than only the Silk Road, because it also involves the building of a corridor along the Trans-Siberian Railway, and

it has many routes going all the way to Indonesia, into Africa. We are really talking about the Silk Road being the beginning of a World Land-Bridge.

And I'm very happy to tell you that my friends in Russia recently communicated to me that while they thought a couple of years ago that this conception would be too big, that now, under the impression of both the dangers in Ukraine, but also the positive experience of Sochi—and I don't mean the Olympic Games, but I mean the fact that Russia has developed the Sochi region as a model for the transformation of other parts of Russia—they are very, very positive about the future perspective of cooperating with the Silk Road, and the Chinese government.

And also, President Putin has expressed very clearly that he seeks such cooperation, so therefore I think there's a very good prospect that this can succeed.

Yang: However, a few days ago, when I was interviewing the Russian Ambassador, Mr. Andrey Avetisyan, he said that what is called the New Silk Road, or economic belt, remains largely a concept. It's not in operation now. At the same, our friends in the Shanghai Cooperation Organization, namely, the Central Asian nations, enjoy very much the Chinese investment. So, do you see the subtle difference in the attitudes of both the Central Asian government, and Russia?

Zepp-LaRouche: Well, I think what counts is the attitude of President Putin, and some of the other people who I'm in contact with, because I don't think that everybody has already moved away from such concerns as the ambassador expressed. Right now we are at an incredibly dangerous moment of history, and either we get our act together as a civilization which can consciously go into a new era of mankind, or we may not exist. If we don't change the way things are going now, we may end up in a Third World War.

So, I think it is extremely important to put a peace order for the 21st Century on the table, and create a level of reason, where everybody who participates has a benefit. So that historical conflicts, past wars, and ethnic conflicts and all these problems are put behind us, because if you build the Eurasian Land-Bridge as a totality, from all of Europe to Asia—

The Central Asian Region

Yang: We must adopt a holistic view about the prospects of the Eurasian Land-Bridge, so you sound very rational, reasonable, and correct.

Perhaps so far we are discussing the prospects of a

Silk Road only from the Russian and Chinese perspective. In this process we may have ignored the important role that the Persian state of Iran plays, because it's a very important littoral state of the Caspian Sea. It enjoys the oil deposits. So, what do you think of the current process of rapprochement between the Western countries and the Islamic Republic of Iran, when it come to energy collaboration between China and the volatile Middle Eastern region?

Zepp-LaRouche: Well, we have created actually a development program as part of the Eurasian Land-Bridge, which encompases the entire region from Afghanistan, Pak-

Creative Commons/Sean O'Flaherty

The World Land-Bridge will make possible the economic development of every nation, Zepp-LaRouche explained. Infrastructure, such as that in Germany (shown here: Hamburg Harbor), "is always the precondition for economic development."

istan, all the way to the Caucasus, to Syria, to the Gulf. To take this region as one area, which right now is torn apart by terrible poverty, by terrorism, by the effects of the drug trade. And if you want to have peace, right now this region is one of the many potential powderkegs which could lead to a Third World War eruption. It's like the Balkan wars before World War I.

The only way to stabilize this region, especially with the perspective of American and NATO troops leaving Afghanistan, or at least a large part of them, you need to put in a real development perspective. And we have developed a program which involves greening the deserts—because most of the region is desert. You can use the water of aquifers. You can redirect certain rivers, which right now flow into the Arctic in Siberia. You can redirect them to the Aral Sea. You can use that water basically to develop all of Central Asia in terms of water. Link pipelines into Iran, and then have as a second phase, the peaceful use of nuclear energy for large demands of desalination of ocean water, and start to green the desert.

We want to put in infrastructure essentially as it is, for example, in western Europe. Germany, for example, enjoys infrastructure which is rivers, railways, highways, which are all interconnected, and infrastructure is always the precondition for economic development.

Yang: Very much so. It is in this area that Chinese investment is highly expected by all the markets in that particular—

Let's look at Afghanistan. It currently remains an observer partner of the Shanghai Cooperation Organization. Following the military drawdown of the U.S. and NATO troops by the end of this year, postwar reconstruction in this landlocked, impoverished country will become a major concern for the rest of the world, as part of the exit strategy, and China will be an integral part of the postwar reconstruction. To my poor knowledge about this country, it used to depend, and perhaps it currently also depends, on drug cultivation and drug trafficking for much of its livelihood. There is also a lot of tribal rivalry between different warlords and landlords and tribal rivalries of different kinds.

What do you think of the difficulties lying ahead for major members of the SCO to get involved in the postwar reconstruction, so that countries along the Silk Road will enjoy true prosperity?

Zepp-LaRouche: The drug production has increased 40 times since NATO started the war in Afghanistan 12 years ago. This has become the major security problem for Russia, which is losing right now 100,000 people per year, and the Russian drug czar, Viktor Ivanov, has called on the West, and other countries, to cooperate to deal with that.

Now, we know that the drug traffic from Afghanistan and the laundering of drug money is the main source for the financing of terrorism, of al-Qaeda, al-Nusra, and similar groupings. But many of the people who have been recruited to this—not because they are radical jihadists, but because they are poor. And if they are offered $500 a month, then they join this, and therefore the key question would be, first to eradicate the drug production—which is very easy: With modern technology you can eradicate it. You can spot the routes of the money laundering. NSA has proven that from satellites, you can spot every plant, if you want, so the question of both stopping the production, and the laundering, is technically no problem.

And then, naturally, you have to put in an alternative, a vast development program for the population, so that they have an incentive to go in a different direction. And I have said for a very long time, if the neighbor countries—Russia, China, Iran, India, Pakistan—would all cooperate in such a regional development conception, then you can get Afghanistan going in a peaceful direction.

But only if you do it as a totality. It does not function if you only take it as one country. There has to be a genuine development of the entire Eurasian Land-Bridge, and then you can contain, and overcome this problem.

Yang: What do you think of the idea of a maritime Silk Road?

Zepp-LaRouche: It's a very good idea, because in Southeast Asia, there is the largest concentration of population in the world, and the present Strait of Malacca, for example, is completely overloaded, and therefore you need to develop new maritime trade routes. For example, we have proposed as part of this Eurasian Land-Bridge, the building of the Kra Canal, which would be parallel to the Strait of Malacca, and open this region for more trade.

If we go in the direction of the Eurasian Land-Bridge, the production of real wealth will increase dramatically, and therefore, you need new trade routes to integrate all of these countries together. And we wrote, for example, many years ago, a plan for a 50-year development of the Pacific region,[1] which already had all of these projects.

But many of these projects are ready to start tomorrow.

---

1. See Lyndon H. LaRouche, Jr., "A 50-year development policy for the Indian-Pacific Oceans Basin," *EIR Special Report*, Sept. 13, 1983.

The Thucydides Trap

Yang: Congratulations. Congratulations on your blueprint, and your vision for the prosperity of the Asian-Pacific region.

So far, I believe you are tyring to look at these issue from the European perspective, which might be acceptable by the parties involved. However, what do you think of the Chinese brainchild of taking over [construction of] the Gwadar deep-water port in Pakistan, and helping construct a port in Myanmar, so that a pipeline could be built to connect the shipments from the seas to Xinjiang, in the case of Pakistan, and through Myanmar to China one way or another?

This is the blueprint of Mr. Xi Jinping and his predecessors.

Zepp-LaRouche: Well, I know that some people may be concerned about China—

Yang: Do you know subcontext for the Chinese brainchildren? Because of the legacy of the Cold War, most Chinese don't quite trust the security umbrella the U.S. provides, because they are afraid of China sharing the center stage in the 21st Century. It's largely a challenge coming from newcomers to the existing international political and economic order. The U.S. is not ready yet; therefore China has to consider its own alternative.

Zepp-LaRouche: But there are also people who say you should not be afraid of the economic prosperity of China. For example, the U.S. Chairman of the Joint Chiefs of Staff, General Martin Dempsey, has made many speeches where he warned the West of falling into the "Thucydides trap." Thucydides was this Greek historian who wrote about the Pelopponesian War, and he said that this war occurred because the Athenians were afraid of the economic growth of Sparta. And he said the growth of China should not lead to such a Thucydides trap.

And in a certain sense, I don't think that is the main problem. The main problem of the world right now is that the entire trans-Atlantic region is collapsing. The U.S. economy is collapsing. The European Union is suffering a terrible crisis in southern Europe. The financial system of the trans-Atlantic region is about to blow out.

Yang: What do you think of the importance of having U.S. support for both a land Silk Road and a maritime Silk Road? Because I hate to always go to geopolitical issues, but don't you think that economic issues and geopolitical issues are quite interwoven?

Creative Commons/Moign Khawaja

Gwadar deep-water port in Pakistan (seen here) is the "brainchild" of China, said Yang Rui, an example of President Xi's blueprint for China's role in the economic development of its neighbors.

Zepp-LaRouche: I think we need to have a change in American policy for it to support the Silk Road. Because right now the United States is not in conformity with its own Constitution, in terms of its policy. There is a lot of criticism of President Obama, even from the Congress, because this is the case, so we need a change in American policy. But there are fortunately many patriots in the country who are thinking exactly about such a change.

We are in a crisis. We are in an existential crisis of civilization right now, and what we are proposing, and President Xi Jinping is proposing, is a vision of the future. And a lot of the geopolitical thinking is of the past. And if you cannot move to the next phase, the next era of civilization, we may not exist.

Right now we are on the verge of World War III. The developments in the Ukraine are extremely dangerous, and could really lead to a terrible confrontation.

Yang: Do you take the political upheaval in Ukraine as a part of their appealing for democratic transformation, or do you think this is largely a geopolitical legacy between the Russians and the European Union, in how to reallocate the political resources in that poor country?

Zepp-LaRouche: No, I think this is the result of a [Western] policy of regime-change, which started when the Soviet Union collapsed. The first phase of this was the Orange Revolution, where the West had put in 2,200 NGOs, which selected a network of people based on their anti-Russian profile. This was in 2004.

But now it's much worse, because what we have now is that the hardcore violence is conducted by Nazis. Svoboda is a Nazi party. They have a swastika as their party logo. And it's completely scandalous that the EU and the United States are supporting such violent networks.

Yang: Well, Ukraine could be part of the broad spectrum of the Silk Road, that goes through Central Asia connecting with much of Europe. Whether the emerging markets or labor markets of the Silk Road will benefit from President Xi Jinping's idea, largely depends on whether the Chinese economy could be sustained, whether we will enjoy sustainable prosperity. So, by the end of this conversation, which I think is very enlightening, what do you think of the future of the Chinese economy, and of the new leadership of President Xi Jinping and Prime Minister Li Keziang?

Zepp-LaRouche: I think they're doing an excellent job. From my standpoint, also Prime Minister Li went to Romania, met with 15 heads of state, and promised that China would build a five-track train system in Eastern and Central Europe. This is all very, very good.

The problem is that the financial system of the trans-Atlantic zone is collapsing. And we need in a change in the monetary system—that's why we propose for the United States and Europe the return to the banking separation which was implemented by President Roosevelt in 1933.

Yang: Thank you for your participation. I truly appreciate it.

President Obama Faces Showdown Over 9/11 Coverup

by Jeffrey Steinberg

April 21—Representatives Walter Jones (R-N.C.) and Stephen Lynch (D-Mass.) wrote to President Obama on April 10, demanding that he finally fulfill his promise to release the classified 28-page chapter from the 2002 Joint Congressional Inquiry into the Sept. 11, 2001 attacks. The two Members of Congress, who have both reviewed the sealed pages, wrote: "The information contained in the redacted pages is critical to U.S. foreign policy moving forward and should thus be available to the American people. Furthermore, the survivors of the 9/11 attacks and families of the victims have waited 12 years to learn all the facts concerning that tragic day. It is my hope that President Barack Obama will recognize the importance of this issue and provide these individuals with the closure that they deserve."

On at least two separate occasions—in February 2009 and September 2011—President Obama personally promised representatives of the 9/11 families that he would declassify and release the 28 pages. But in the five years that he has served as President, he has continued to reneg on that promise.

Jones and Lynch made clear that they believe that no national security damage would be caused by releasing the pages at this time. "Having read the classified information," they wrote, "we believe that releasing it will not cause harm to U.S. intelligence sources and methods. Indeed, we consider this to be a matter of providing the American people with all the facts regarding 9/11 and bringing closure to the many individuals who lost family and friends in the attacks or survived the attacks themselves."

The letter reminded the President that they had introduced House Resolution 428, urging the release of the classified pages, and that the resolution has bipartisan support in the House and has the full endorsement of former Sen. Bob Graham (D-Fla.), who chaired the Joint inquiry and has fought for the declassification of the 28 pages ever since.

The pressure on President Obama to live up to his promise is building on other fronts as well. On April 18, Federal District Court Judge William Zloch gave the FBI until April 25 to deliver an estimated 92,000 documents on the 9/11 investigation conducted by the Sarasota, Fla., FBI office. The judge is presiding over a Freedom of Information Act (FOIA) lawsuit by the *Broward Bulldog* newspaper, demanding FBI files on their investigation into Esam Ghazzawi, a Saudi national with close ties to the Saudi royal family, who hosted several of the 9/11 hijackers at his Florida home, including Mohammed Atta, the presumed leader of the terror team.

Ghazzawi, a wealthy Saudi businessman and advisor to members of the Saudi royal family, also hosted Adnan Shukrijumah, a fugitive al-Qaeda leader for whom the FBI has offered a $5 million reward. Days before the 9/11 attacks, Ghazzawi and his family abruptly left their home in a secured gated community and fled the United States, leaving behind cars, clothing, and almost all of their belongings. The story of the Ghazzawi links to Atta and two other 9/11 hijackers was broken by the *Broward Bulldog* in 2011, and the paper filed an FOIA suit to access the exhaustive FBI files on the incident.

The FBI failed to inform the Joint Congressional Committee about their probe of the Sarasota cell, despite numerous document requests to the Bureau. Now, Judge Zloch has insisted on seeing the documents for judicial review.

In his ruling, Judge Zloch wrote that "Defendant's eagerness to assert exemptions and wooden method of interpreting Plaintiff's [FOIA] requests essentially deprives the court of its role in examining any relevant documents and independently determining whether any exemptions may apply."

Saudi Arabia's Liability

In yet another blow to the Bush-Cheney and Obama coverup of 9/11, the U.S. Supreme Court is expected to take up an appeal by the Kingdom of Saudi Arabia to reinstate sovereign immunity in a series of Federal court cases holding Riyadh accountable for the 9/11 attacks. If the Supreme Court refuses to grant the Saudi Kingdom this exemption from legal action, the entire 9/11 coverup could be blown apart.

In one lawsuit by an international insurance company, Lloyds of London, against the Kingdom of Saudi Arabia, investigators provided a 125-page documentary brief on how various Saudi charities and ministries provided tens of millions of dollars to finance al-Qaeda's global operations during the period leading up to the 9/11 attacks. Although the suit was withdrawn on technical, jurisdictional grounds, it stands as a stunning indictment of the multiple dimensions of Saudi official financing of the global jihadist terror apparatus behind the 9/11 attacks and scores of other atrocities.

The Impeachable Obama

Senator Graham has drawn a strong parallel between the Bush-Cheney and Obama coverup of the 9/11 funding by Saudi Arabia and the ongoing Obama coverup of the CIA's torture/renditions program throughout the post-9/11 period.

The responsibility for what the intelligence agencies do rests with the President, now Barack Obama, Graham declared in an interview on the <u>Real News Network</u> posted March 17. Graham was asked for his views of the dispute between the CIA and the Senate Intelligence Committee. Graham said that in the current torture scandal, the intelligence agencies covered up things and didn't keep the Committee informed, as in the case of the two future 9/11 hijackers in San Diego who were living in the home of an FBI informant, and who had close ties to Saudi government agents.

When the interviewer asked him about what some people call the "deep state," the idea that "the intelligence institutions have really their own momentum and agenda," Graham replied that the responsibility is on the President who appoints the leadership of the intelligence agencies. "I don't assume that these are just rogue people out doing whatever they want to. I assume that they are acting at the direction of the President."

The interviewer then noted that in the case of the torture program, this was Bush and Cheney, but now, with the 6,000-page Senate torture report, it is Obama, and he could declassify it today, if he wanted to. Graham responded: "As you know, there is another, similar situation involving our report of the 9/11, where there was a chapter of 28 pages which largely deals with the question of who financed 9/11. That chapter has been censored now for more than 12 years, and there is no evidence that there is any likelihood that it's going to be made available to the American people in the near future. I think that's an outrage. There's nothing in that report that involves today's national security. There is a lot in that report which might help explain how did 9/11—how was it allowed and capable of actually occurring? And that information should be available to the American people."

The interviewer then brought up the McClatchy report on Obama withholding from the Senate 6,000 pages of documents related to the torture investigation. As to how this will play out, Graham put the onus on Obama: "The President is inevitably going to be the ultimate figure in how this matter is resolved. I personally hope that he will resolve it on the side of openness, and then be prepared to deal with the consequences of letting the American people know what's happening, and that it won't be just limited, as important as it is, to this 6,000-page report on torture, that it will also include things like the report on who financed 9/11."

Does anyone think that anything short of Obama's impeachment will compel release of the suppressed pages, as Graham is demanding?

Rogers Campaign Evokes Americans' Optimistic Spirit

by Harley Schlanger

April 22—In several recent discussions, Lyndon La-Rouche has emphasized that the solution to the present deadly crises confronting mankind requires both telling the truth about the causes of the crises, and offering real solutions. Following this advice has been the reason for the momentum building around the U.S. Senate campaign of LaRouche Democrat Kesha Rogers, as she and her campaign have made sure that a growing number of Texas voters recognize her as the candidate leading the drive to impeach President Obama, for his role as an agent of a foreign power—the Anglo-Dutch-Saudi Empire—working to destroy the U.S.

Rogers' role in leading the drive for impeachment has led the declining number of Obama supporters in Texas to engage in an almost ritualistic, whining chant, "She is not a Democrat." Even the usually pro-Obama *Austin American Statesman* "Political Fact Finder" column concluded that this impotent slander against Rogers is "false."

With the April 12 conference on Ending the Drought, co-sponsored by Rogers and her fellow LaRouche Democrat Michael Steger, who is running against Nancy Pelosi in San Francisco, the campaign demonstrated that the candidate is presenting the solution to the crises (see cover story, this issue). The conference took on the underlying cultural and scientific problems which underlie the crises: the anti-human ideology of the so-called Green movement, which, combined with the "fiscal conservatism" preached by both parties, have brought the U.S. to the point of collapse of both the physical economy, and of the bloated, speculative financial bubble built on its corpse.

Rogers and Steger presented how different the world could be, if the scientific and cultural principles of the Golden Renaissance governed the policies of nations today. It was those principles which accounted for the American Revolution—against the Anglo-Dutch Empire—and our republican Constitution, and for the periods of fantastic scientific and technological progress, when those principles were applied, by the few Presidents who understood them. They spoke of the genius of Alexander Hamilton and his credit policy, of the continental nation-building of John Quincy Adams and Abraham Lincoln, and of the 20th-Century revival of those principles and ideals under Franklin Roosevelt and John F. Kennedy.

Reviving FDR and JFK

Those Presidents, Rogers has been emphasizing, understood that our nation remained at war with the British Empire. Hamilton, Lincoln, and Ken-

EIRNS/Sylvia Spaniolo

Kesha Rogers' campaign for Senate in Texas has challenged politics as usual with her fighting spirit, and begun to turn around the pessimism in the electorate. She is shown here at the Houston Rodeo parade in March.

nedy were all murdered by British agents. Our last two Presidents, George Bush, Jr. and Barack Obama, have been puppets of that same British Empire. But, she concluded, with our campaigns, we can destroy that Empire, and the Wall Street and City of London bankers who run it, and rebuild America as the nation that the rest of the world once looked up to with boundless admiration.

In the last two weeks, preceding the conference and after, Rogers has taken this message across the state. She campaigned in the Dallas-Fort Worth area, in Austin, San Antonio, and El Paso. In each location, she was interviewed by reporters, some of whom reported what she actually said, rather than just printing the Obama Democrats' lies against her. In a series of "Meet and Greets" in these cities, longtime supporters mingled with some who had just met her campaign organizers, and joined together in mapping out a strategy to win the runoff election on May 27.

What is motivating those joining the campaign is its spirit that is generated by the candidate. Whether discussing how FDR took on the crooked bankers on Wall Street with Glass-Steagall, or how Kennedy took on the Malthusians with his fight for scientific and technological progress, Rogers is never pedantic, but works to bring out the deeply buried optimistic spirit in those beaten down by the induced cynicism of our times, and the wretched economic conditions through which most are suffering.

In discussing, for example, how implementing the full, thermonuclear design for NAWAPA XXI will not just address the drought and create the necessary nonlinear jump in energy-flux density required to increase productivity to provide for the more than 7 billion people on Earth today, but will offer hope to young people who are otherwise suffering through a nonproductive existence, Rogers is inspiring people to imagine a better future, one which they can play a part in creating.

Alameel's Money Can't Buy Him Love!

The excited response Rogers has been evoking has led nervous Democratic hacks to realize that they cannot allow her opponent in the Democratic runoff, Wall Street millionaire David Alameel, to hide behind his wall of money. Alameel's millions could not buy a Congressional nomination in 2012, nor could he buy the Senate nomination this March. As his refusal to face Rogers in debate is embarrassing the Obama operatives

sent to Texas, who wished to use him and his money to at least appear competitive, he has been sent out on a tour to make a few tightly controlled public appearances.

This led to a disaster for Alameel in San Antonio, when he was asked repeatedly by Rogers supporters in LULAC (League of United Latin American Citizens), at the Cesar Chavez parade, why he will not debate. His pathetic response, that "she is not a Democrat," met with derision. On April 20, he was further exposed when Rogers confronted him on an El Paso radio interview, asking him why he goes along with Obama's destructive policies. Alameel was again reduced to mumbling the "not a Democrat" defense, leading the radio host to invite Rogers to appear on his program next week.

One of the more significant failures of the Obama operatives and Texas Democratic Party hacks has been their transparent efforts to buy the Hispanic vote. Alameel has been ridiculed in a popular blog run by a LULAC activist, Voice of the Mainland, for his effort to win support from Hispanics by financing "ghost" councils of LULAC. The crude exclusion of Rogers, by a political ally of Alameel's (i.e., a recipient of his funds) to prevent her from speaking at a Dallas-area LULAC meeting, to which she had been invited, led to several invitations from other councils, whose members are hungry for discussion of issues, ranging from the war danger and immigration to jobs, housing, health care, etc.—none of which can be addressed by Wall Street puppet and Obama defender Alameel.

In contrast, doors are being opened to the Rogers campaign. On Easter Sunday, the priest at the St. Ignatius Catholic Church invited the Rogers campaigners there to set up a booth outside the church, and allowed a representative to speak to nearly 1,000 parishioners about the war danger. Her April 19 address to a Houston LULAC chapter was warmly received, even by one who initially greeted her by saying, "I hate LaRouche."

With five weeks left until the runoff vote, it is now conceivable that Rogers can win. And that would be a profound blow to those clinging to the declining figure of Barack Obama, as well as to the Bushies in the GOP in Texas, who are hoping that a defeat of Rogers by the hapless millionaire Alameel—who once contributed great sums to them—would allow them to sweep, once again, all the statewide offices in the Lone Star State.

BACK TO REAL SCIENCE!

The Incompetence of Twentieth-Century Science Education

by Lyndon H. LaRouche, Jr.

March 28, 2014

A great, and largely continuing catastrophe for all modern science throughout the world, had begun, in Paris, France, since the opening of the Twentieth Century. It had been was launched by a scientifically weak-minded David Hilbert, delivered from the platform of that Year 1900's **International Mathematical Congress**, held in Paris at that time.

The foolish Hilbert had abandoned, and implicitly rejected, all actual physical science. He had done that for the sake of a silly pursuit of a merely mathematics program, without any actual physical science, thus abandoning, and implicitly outlawing all competent progress in physical science. From that time onwards, trans-Atlantic science has been, and that chiefly increasingly so, an often, actually criminal farce, perpetrated against the very name of a polluted, mere caricature of actual science, a fraud conducted in the favor of what was, to repeat, "merely mathematics."

The travesty which had begun with David Hilbert's particular hoax, had launched that year of sheer evils, 1900 A.D. This was, then, soon to be followed by Hilbert's, far more evil successor, indeed, the most evil man of the Twentieth Century (and beyond), Bertrand Russell. Unfortunately, the teaching and practice of the underlying, morally wretched principles of practiced attempts at mere mathematics, have, since, tended to persist, as still presently, as a demanded replacement, in high schools and universities, that for nearly all, but a dwindling handful of true geniuses, which have survived to have been engaged in truly competent modern science, still presently.

What the unfortunate Hilbert had already done to this effect, had, thus, become, soon, a greatly worsened product, then, but even still later, all that at an accelerated rate.[1] This offense against the forward progress of human nature itself, has been worsened, since that time, by the added evil of a dominant role of the increasing trend toward incompetence in generally practiced methods of what is often only merely taught as so-called science (increasingly in merely mathematics), up to the present date.

All of this had been done under the presently still continuing decadence of a Bertrand Russell who, even still even deader than dead today, reigns in tradition, despite all else, still among the ranks of the reigning royal degenerates of Great Britain, as being their continuing worship of the virtual Satans of pseudo-science, ever since, all the way to the presently royally imperial day. The product of all this, has been, to the present date, a virtual reincarnation of the "Whore of Babylon," for the practice of science, in every respect, as so to be

Bertrand Russell, whom LaRouche calls "the most evil man of the Twentieth Century (and beyond)," did more than any other person to propagate the abandonment of actual science in favor of the farce of "merely mathematics."

judged to be so, by her reigning deeds, still today.

Over the course of the period from the early 1960s, up to the present time, the collapse of even a formerly taught commitment to a continuing general improvement in the competence in the application of physical science, had been rudely, even savagely, reversed, that somewhat by such a silly fool as Hilbert, but, then, rabidly, by the outrightly satanic Bertrand Russell, who has soon virtually gobbled-up the appeal of the pathetic fool, Hilbert. Since then, the consequent of "green" incompetence, has become a dogma of folly now often predominant in even our own universities generally,

1. Since the cancellation of President Franklin Roosevelt's Glass-Steagall law.

even often as a virtually predominant trend in education and related practices; this has been continued as recently accelerating toward a relative nadir, through to the present date. The practical application of real science approaches zero; economic productivity of trans-Atlantic nations has already long been running in the negative.

That same pollution in scientific opinion has not only remained dominant to the present date, but has been greatly worsened, again, and yet again, in the halls of our Congress, and other influential institutions, despite some important, even precious minorities of exceptions, to the present time.

The Effects on Society

The effects of that same reductionists' counter-revolution against any remaining margin of competence in science, as also in morals and science alike, which had been led, originally, by Hilbert, from Paris, and then, with a literally Satanic forcefulness, by Russell. The result has been a general, long wave of economic decline since the very birth of the Twentieth Century, that done in favor of mere number-systems, *per capita*, to the present date. This had been done, as the sheer evil which the Roman Empire had crafted earlier, but, now chiefly at the behest of the British imperial monarchy which had already led a permanent state of global world-wide wars and related atrocities, since the ouster of he who had been the leading peacekeeper of Europe, Chancellor Bismarck.

The convenient assassination of a great U.S. President, William McKinley, done by a treasonously disposed British imperial asset, the Theodore Roosevelt sodden with the worship of the slave-system's traditions, had set into motion a series of economically declining U.S. Presidencies, which, but for two exceptions, President Taft, and one eliminated by assassination,[2] until President Franklin D. Roosevelt in 1932-1933. A worse, politically motivated situation for the United States, than ever before, has followed the close of the incumbency of President William Clinton: thus unleashing a plunge into the worst tyrannies of our U.S. Presidency to present date, all of which has been done since President Clinton's retirement, all the way to the present instance of chaotically plunging productivity and standards of living.

History in Motion

While the statement which I have just made, above, is true beyond any actually reasonable considerations, the fact of this matter could not be effectively understood, without first examining the process which has actually caused this presently dismal effect upon the minds of mankind generally, a decadence now still proceeding at an accelerating rate over the successive terms of office of, first, Vice-President Dick Cheney, and, accelerated on the scale of wild-eyed economic and moral degeneracy, greatly worsened since the Presidency of a frankly evil Barack Obama.

In fact, since approximately the beginning of the present year, 2014, the U.S. economy has been plunging into a hopelessly desperate, Wall Street-led general bankruptcy, that under an accelerating financial breakdown crisis with the present characteristics of the infamous Weimar breakdown-crisis of post-World War I Germany. To wit: the so-called, present state of Wall Street and London panic conditions, now existing under the present, so-called "bail-in" conditions.[3]

Now, something much worse has happened recently:

The recent reopening of the sessions of the U.S. Congress have begun with an outburst of what is, effectively, hysterical fits of raw political-economic fear, a condition which has driven many members of the U.S. Congress into strategic-economic clinical bursts of moral inanities. Wall Street "money" is, as a matter of course, a principal, inherently poisonous stimulant for this shameful behavior. There is much which must be immediately changed on that account. I present, below, first, a few choice high-lights of that case, here, now, that the evil may be diagnosed, and, therefore, remedied. After that, I shall turn, gradually, to the actually scientific meat of the matter.

My following subject here, is, therefore: the principle of what is, and shall be, actually physical science: as it represents the true measure of true human progress.

Prelude: The Human Species

The subject of a competent science, is to be limited, essentially, and ultimately, to the difference which separates the human species, from all other, presently known, living species.

The simplest efficient choice for setting a standard for this feature of the human species' existence, would be the specifically willful expression of increased, physically efficient power, *per-capita*, as that is uniquely characteristic of the human species, as through the means of the effects of advancement in, chiefly, practiced chemistry: the power, to increase the power, *per capita*, of the members of the human species, through increasing the effective energy-flux-density supplied to the aid of the human will, as this may be measured per capita: which is a measurable standard for defining the meaning of human progress.[4]

At the same time, we must take into account, the fact, that the human species has experienced a division, chiefly, between two sub-categories: the evil "Zeusian," versus the "Promethean." The Zeusian type is the morally degenerate type; the Promethean type is the viable type which expresses the mode of the naturally progressive growth and increased energy-flux density of the human population. For example, the Roman and British empires are prominent among the category of the Zeusian types.[5] The Zeusian mode, e.g., the Roman and British empires, are typical of the intrinsically degenerate varieties of human cultures.

2. Warren G. Harding 1921-1923, died, allegedly of eating oysters while rail-roading across the great western desert.

3. If the British Empire were to have provoked a general thermonuclear war before the effects of the present "bail-in" gamble were to strike down the present global economic system, the British imperial scheme for global genocide might meet the requirements of the present British Empress's stated strategic, policy intentions. However, if the general thermonuclear warfare were delayed until after the "bail-in" breakdown, the British empire itself would itself be virtually wiped out, first! Hence the panicked present intent for a virtually "World War III," by such as the brutish Queen's own U.S. puppet, President Barack Obama. Hence, Obama's desperate demand for thermonuclear World War III.

4. As measured in terms of increase of relative energy-flux density.

5. See the case of Edward Gibbon, re: **The Decline and Fall of The Roman Empire**.

FIGURE 1

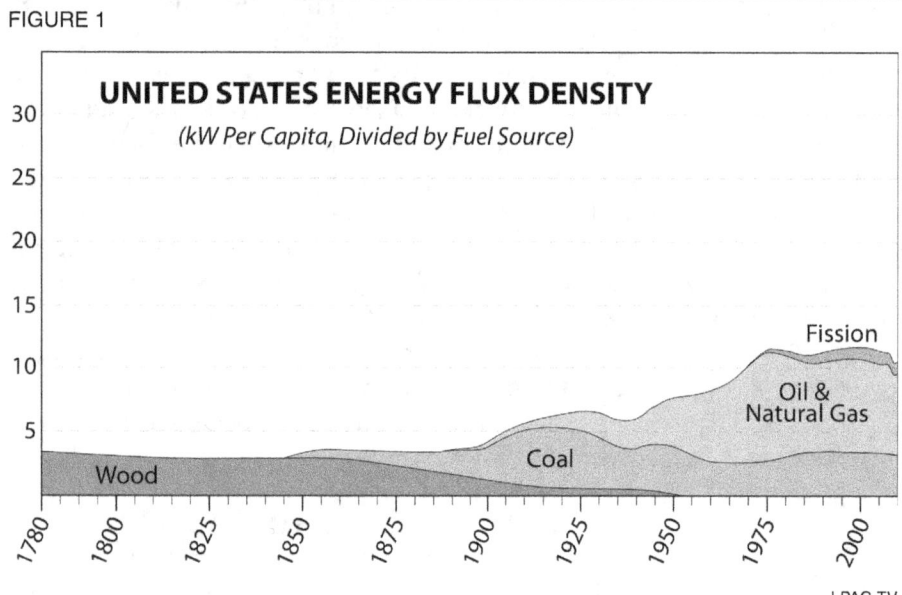

UNITED STATES ENERGY FLUX DENSITY
(kW Per Capita, Divided by Fuel Source)

LPAC-TV

Energy-flux density measures not just energy usage, but the rate of energy usage, per capita or per area of national territory. The rise in energy-flux density occurs through leaps in man's power in and over the universe.

For the purpose of illustrating the significance of that unique quality of the human, specifically *noëtic* will, I shall focus my attention here, provisionally, on some aspects from the earlier history of our human cultures; but, much of that is done here merely to situate the relevant record of human process in the history of modern times: which is to say, since the great ecumenical achievements typified by the effects of the leadership supplied by three outstanding personalities now identified, together with the more notably relevant followers into recent, modern times of continuing change:

First, to begin that specific account, for the benefit of those who had missed my earlier account, I refresh, once more, my earlier outline of the original general case for a truly modern science launched since the beginning of the Renaissance led by Filippo Brunelleschi, Nicholas of Cusa, and Johannes Kepler:[6]

The Birth of Modern Trans-Atlantic Civilization

In my immediately preceding, most recent reports on the subject of the modern history of physical science's progress,[7] I had presented, as repeatedly as nec-

essary, a two-phased account of revolutionary improvements in the applied principles of physical science, as follows: (1) The unified common principle of Brunelleschi, Nicholas of Cusa, and Johannes Kepler; and, (2) the role of the successive steps in progress of Nineteenth-Century physical science typified by the revolutionary, successive steps toward a Nineteenth-century, new scientific revolution prepared, most crucially, by Carl Friedrich Gauss and his follower, Bernhard Riemann, the latter since Riemann's own, thoroughly revolutionary, June 10, 1854 habilitation dissertation.[8]

I have already emphasized in an immediately earlier report, that the consequence of those and related stages reflect a precise notion of a progressive development of actually modern physical science, as over the course, in net effect, from the Renaissance typified by the signal achievements of the continuity of (1) Brunelleschi, Cusa, and Kepler, in the actual defining of modern European physical science, which have persisted in their beneficial effects, since then, as I have emphasized on a recent occasion. This has been a continued progress, through the subsequent

---

com/lar/2014/4113satan_russells_corpse.html,

8. Notably: Gauss had been sitting in attendance for his protege's (Riemann's) famous, 1854, habilitation dissertation; however, the originality of what Riemann had achieved on that occasion, did much to illustrate, this time, more fully, the unique measures which had been already taken by Gauss himself. Riemann's own work, on that occasion, and following it to the end of his own life, was, in turn, the foundation for the successive, complementary, and actually definitive, revolutionary achievements made by Max Planck and Albert Einstein. With the Paris atrocity led by David Hilbert in 1900, and the ensuing criminality against science led by Bertrand Russell across most of the span of the Twentieth Century, science has made, despite all else, some notable progress based on the foundations of the Gauss-Riemann and Planck-Einstein trends in Nineteenth Century science; but, the practice of that progress had already been collapsing in rate with, most notably, with the assassination of President John F. Kennedy, and collapsed, in net effect, with the near-impeachment of President William Clinton. The "Green" doctrine, created by the British Empire's influence, has virtually destroyed the remaining elements of viability in the U.S.A. and European economies, in net effect, most emphatically, that immediately on the inauguration of the Presidency of the essentially silly, if also nasty, George W. Bush, Jr.

---

6. I refer repeatedly to those cases, unavoidably, throughout this report.
7. Lyndon H. LaRouche, Jr. **The Satan Still Operating From Inside Bertrand Russell's Corpse**, March 19, 2014. http://www.larouchepub.

influence of Gauss and Riemann in preparing the ground for the comparably significant achievements of (2) Max Planck and Albert Einstein, and, prospectively, still, V.I. Vernadsky's intention for his excellent, but uncompleted dedication to the future progress of physical science as a whole, presently. As I have noted on earlier occasions, the completed perspective for the future of mankind's development now, depends upon the proximate perfection of the legacy of the great specialist in scoping out the implications of the principle of life, *per se*, that of the same V.I. Vernadsky.

These foregoing cases are the recurring point of reference to matters of principle, throughout this report as a whole.

The continuing development of that introductory phase of the present series of reports on this matter, as by me, and, I think, a number from among my own collaborators, and by, hopefully, other scientific thinkers, have already known, or might be known to me, otherwise, as well. Once the evil "chains of illusion" were broken, we will have been given cause to be hopeful respecting mankind's prospects for more advanced knowledge of the future: a kind of putting to an end of the matter which might be conjectured as conclusive by such as any nasty little Rumpelstiltskin.[9]

Satan & His Money

Take the case of President Abraham Lincoln's method for his success in defeating the British empire's slave-holding puppet: "greenbacks." Wall Street and kindred forms of money-transactions were (wonderfully) driven bankrupt by President Lincoln's action for a currency based on the banking authority of the U.S. Treasury: that is how the U.S.A. defeated the British Empire's stooges from outside and inside the borders of our republic during the course of the U.S. Civil War.

It was already all there in our original Federal Republic. Original Treasury Secretary Alexander Hamilton had already clarified the principle of our Republic's success. "Simply money," such as Wall Street money generally, has actually no intrinsic value, still (actually) today; Wall Street today is, now, far worse than hopelessly bankrupt. With the arrival of the British-Wall Street situation as of the beginning of this present year, the shift from "bail-out," to "bail-in," there is no intrinsic value, whatsoever, in Wall Street's money; it is all, intrinsically, worthless already: *Pfft!* Hence, the urgency of the current international war-drive.

The true wealth of society – almost any society – exists only in the increase of the actually productive powers of labor. Wall Street's claims are essentially worth much-much less than money; it is, chiefly, no more than the ill-gotten gains extorted from the helpless or, worse, the foolish, by an international system of organized crime, such as the present British Empire and its organized-crime chieftain of the moment, the current Brutish Empress, Elizabeth.[10]

Wall Street's and London system is, from top, to bottom, remains the true "steal business."

The fraud (the swindle) of U.S.A. and European contemporary financial buggery, reposes, ultimately, in nothing more, or less than the timidity, or sheer ignorance, of the commonly credulous. As productive employment has been taken away from the citizens of the United States, more and more, since Wall Street's implicit rape of the American economic system, and that with a corresponding, political and practical worthlessness among the citizenry.

This has become, currently, a trend which has, increasingly, reduced the older generations of formerly proud producers to holders of a virtual beggar's bowl, a bowl ever more and more empty, especially since the sheer brutality against our citizens by the Cheney and, even more drastically, the Obama administration. Even what might be considered as the powers of the U.S. Congress are drooling, mostly piteously, at the verge of the beggar's bowl of Wall Street tyrannies: a Wall Street, itself, is now seemingly, about to crush virtually out of continued existence by the greatest financial crash in all actually known history to date.[11]

9. A children's-story substitute for the too frightening image of a likeness of an actual Satan, or an Adolf Hitler. As for Obama, most citizens already hate him, with good reasons. (Never fear, so far, they will express rage; but, there has been a fear to do anything more useful than that mere posturing.) Simple impeachment is what is actually warranted in this case; but, Wall Street and its butt-kissers, including members of Congress seeking funding for re-election, are still licking the rumps of hoped-for a immanently bankrupt Wall Street's largesse (not only Republicans!).

10. Nominally, today: the actually current Empress Elizabeth II. (In historical fact), and with respect to peculiarities of temperament, the real, earlier monarch, Elizabeth I, was the actual predecessor (by her own characteristic intentions), as a matter manifestly efficient, physical principle. Shakespeare had effectively understood the relevant practice and its effects, alike.

11. I remind the readers, that if the U.S.A. were to adopt three principal

In any competent conduct of a monetary system, money as such has never had any intrinsic economic value, in effect; value is to be measured in terms of *only* the effective increase, of the physical-productive powers of labor of a society as such: not labor *per se*, but, rather that of the productive powers of labor, as defined in the four crucial, founding principles of the U.S. National Economy defined by Secretary of the Treasury Alexander Hamilton. Any contrary opinion, is simply, more or less badly incompetent, merely that of a monetarist expression of public economic masturbation. In brief: both Wall Street and London are, and always had been, essentially, worthless frauds.

Evils of such likenesses, whether relatively less, or worse, are familiar from within the skein of known human history. However, now, the planet is lurking at the edge of the threat of a general thermonuclear war, a war, which were it to occur now, as is presently already threatened: this would mean either the sudden extermination—even (presently) as if in about an hour and half: or, a Zeus-like ancient Rome or contemporary British empire, either of which would possess the sheer evil of such intentions; throughout the planet, of the present human species as such, or an unprecedented holocaust, during

"Saturn Devouring His Son," by Francisco Goya (ca. 1819-23). Not Zeus, but one of his satanic cohorts: a "Monster of Sheer Evil."

which the survivors would have wished that they, had better died, than continued to live. This is the true image of the evil of the Zeus who has been the proper image of a Monster of Sheer Evil, so seemingly distinguished as a relatively greatest force for evil, from among all the greatest known reigns of human life, to the present time.

Such images, such as the legendary Zeus, are the models, such as those of Zeus, the Roman Empire, and the present-day British Empire: they are essentially models for any actual Satan, who might care to make such investments. They have been, and remain, models for the ultimately, more or less, self-extinctions of empires, empires either known, or only as footprints from an obscured past, heretofore. So far, here, I have left much to be explained in the course of the following chapters.

I. Mind Versus Sense-Perception

Let us, now, therefore, return to the earlier subject of science as redefined in exemplary ways by the models of the true greatest geniuses of the Florentine Renaissance, taken in order of appearance: (1) Brunelleschi, (2) Nicholas of Cusa, and the indispensable achievements by their follower, (3) Johannes Kepler. The competence of all modern science depends upon the specifically combined contributions of those three greatest (actually), from among the inaugural intellects of modern European history at that time.

The essential distinction of honest human beings, from beasts and usurers alike, is that the human species' existence had lain in the potential and actual foundations of all great scientific achievements since the "dark ages" this far. The characteristic of a valid human effort,

---

reforms immediately, the beginning of a recovery of the U.S. Economy would begin immediately. These are, in order of appearance of the actions: (1) The immediate restoration of President Franklin Roosevelt's exact Glass-Steagall Law; (2) The mandatory requirement that no bank shall be authorized under law, except through the authority of the U.S. Treasury (exactly as President Abraham Lincoln had done during the Civil War fought against the British Empire); (3) A Federal Credit funded system of public works based on an orientation under high rates of energy-flux density reconstruction and related measures, and science-driver oriented public works and public education and health-care.

has always been the increase of the energy-flux-density commanded by commitment to accord with the noëtic principles which absolutely distinguishes the characteristics of the human species, from all other presently known creatures. Already, that potential had freed the willing human minds associated with such manifest characteristics, by freeing mankind from the inherently degrading mental slavery of foolishly blinded faith in the ultimate silliness of what is merely sense-perception.

The Global Prospect

My emphasis, here, on the trans-Atlantic cultures, when it is appropriately referenced, is not exclusive, but merely, necessarily, paradigmatic. For example, if we divide the human population of the planet in a meaningful way, the dominant characteristics of the human populations of our planet had been, since the Great Renaissance: the impact for progress of the colonization of the Americas, particularly in the Northern Hemisphere. It had been the freedom of the early American settlements, which had been the indispensable, great drivers of the consequent progress in Europe, generally, as the great German Chancellor Bismarck had learned that great lesson from close study of the then ongoing leadership of the President Abraham Lincoln administration.[12]

However, since the death of the U.S.A.'s President Franklin Roosevelt, there had been a net downward-turning trend, which had been continued as a set of successions of decline, and plunge into a critical phase, in the trans-Atlantic region, since the assassination of the virtual Presidential candidate, Robert Kennedy, the brother of the already assassinated President John F. Kennedy. A similar attempted assassination had been made against President Ronald Reagan, that with clearly identifiable motive for that aborted attempt: we in the United States had thus entered "the Bush League" consequent upon, also, the foul legacy of the influence of the Dulles brothers and their like.

The down-turn in the United States, which has been in net progress downward, since the assassination of John F. Kennedy, has been carried over into the follies induced within western and central Europe.[13] There was nothing necessary in this downward trend throughout the trans-Atlantic-Western European sector; it was a downward dictated by the British Empire under the imperial reign of the Empress Elizabeth, a process of imperial tyranny under the British Empire akin to the precedent of 'The Decline and Fall of the Roman Empire," a willfully (actually *Zeusian*) characteristic of all actually imperialist systems known to ancient through modern mankind presently.

The effect of the decline in the trans-Atlantic region, which has been caused, essentially, by the influence of the present British Empire, has left a relative political-economic value of slightly upward development, as in India and China, for example. This digression has brought a current zest, imported from the ever-evil British Empire, for a presently lively prospect, for a global thermonuclear war.

However, the natural tendency in the history of the human species, when not under the thumb of empires in the actually *Zeusian* tradition, is *Promethean*.

That is not merely a political fact, it is a natural fact: the conflict between the tradition of Zeus and that of Prometheus, reflects a conflict between the *Zeusian* (inherently degenerate) and *Promethean* (creative) modes of organized human populations.

Thus, a Promethean tendency within Russia, India, and China (for example), is now the issue which prompts the British-Empire-dominated, still implicitly Zeusian sector of the planet, in opposition to that Promethean tendency shown significantly in the progressively upward direction of the core elements of the Promethean leaning in the Asian sector. This, however, has been continually challenged from within the Eurasian strategic sector, since the two Chechen wars against Russia whose ravages include, consequently, the British-led use of Saudi terrorist forces in such cases as the so-called British-Saudi-backed "9-11" terror attack on the United States, a mass-murder of U.S. Citizens and others, which was covered over, largely, through the implicitly treasonous actions of U.S. Vice-President

---

12. It had been the role of Chancellor Bismarck which had blocked the persistent threat of what was to become "World War I." It had been the ouster of Bismarck by the actions of the British monarchy's intervention for the ouster of Bismarck, which had immediately unloosed, with the ensuing assassination of the President of France, the virtually continuous two decades and a half of assorted warfare, orchestrated by imperial London, leading into "The Guns of August." Warfare between World Wars I, II, and now imminently threatened III (global thermonuclear), have been merely transitions in a continuing series of conflicts.

13. The decline and ouster of France's President Charles de Gaulle, turned France into a political sewer of British-directed so-called "socialism." from which the entirety of western continental Europe has never actually recovered, to the present date.

Dick Cheney, and as continued by President Barack Obama, both on behalf of the British empire of Queen Elizabeth, as such.

II. Since the Renaissance

The language-cultures of those great, still surviving cultures of that region, can be traced to a convergence of insight among the relatively most successful language-cultures, there, as in the world more broadly. The medium's differences, are often in essential respects of usages; but the progress of physical science, in the highest meaning of that term, is, or, should be, convergent among them, and, hopefully, successfully, as in the best nations of Eurasia, from the western borders of Russia and its immediate associates, today, to the Pacific coasts of Asia today.

Yet, it must be acknowledged, that there are relatively good and bad cultures among the totality of the assortments, the worst of which have been expressions of what have been, inherently, murderously inclined, religious fanaticisms, such as those cases fostered since the religious warfare in Europe, and beyond, since the crushing of what is namable as that "Golden Renaissance" expressed by such as Brunelleschi, Nicholas of Cusa, and Johannes Kepler: those three geniuses must be considered as crucially seminal intellectual forces in action since the birth of the great European Renaissance coming out of preceding, mass-murderous, European "Dark Age."

Zeus Against the Renaissance

Mass murder in the name of religion, when taken in the alleged pursuit of religious fanaticism, such as the fascism, murderous religious fanaticism, or similar brutishness, has sometimes dominated modern European cultures, and others. These are typical of the evils which a true scientific practice must extinguish for the sake of humanity itself. Those murderous fanatics of terrorism, whether inside regions of Europe, or elsewhere, must be subjected to the governing reigns of truly human law, as I shall deal with that subject-matter in the due course of this presently continuing report.

Inspiration, such as religious inspiration, without the same truly human, scientific reason expressed by the original Christian martyrs and their like, is an expression of the essentially evil spirit of the fanaticism of

Mass murder in the name of religion: the Spanish Inquisition. This painting by Pedro Berruguete shows "Saint Dominic Presiding Over an Auto-Da-Fé" (1475).

a Zeusian-like Satan himself, and the British imperial monarchy of today, too, as it should be recognized, exactly so, among all the truly civilized nations generally. It is proof of the goodness of the cultures of mankind which is required, when intended for the commonly future benefit of all nations, which is the only proper universal principle of government.

The only civilized differences among the worthy nations of this planet, pertain to the essential role of what can be fairly, by definition, as language-cultures. The means, not the conventional meanings of mere words as such; those words, as such, are merely the footprints left behind by the passage of time. Truly Classical artistic composition, including science and great classical language-cultures, should never be de-

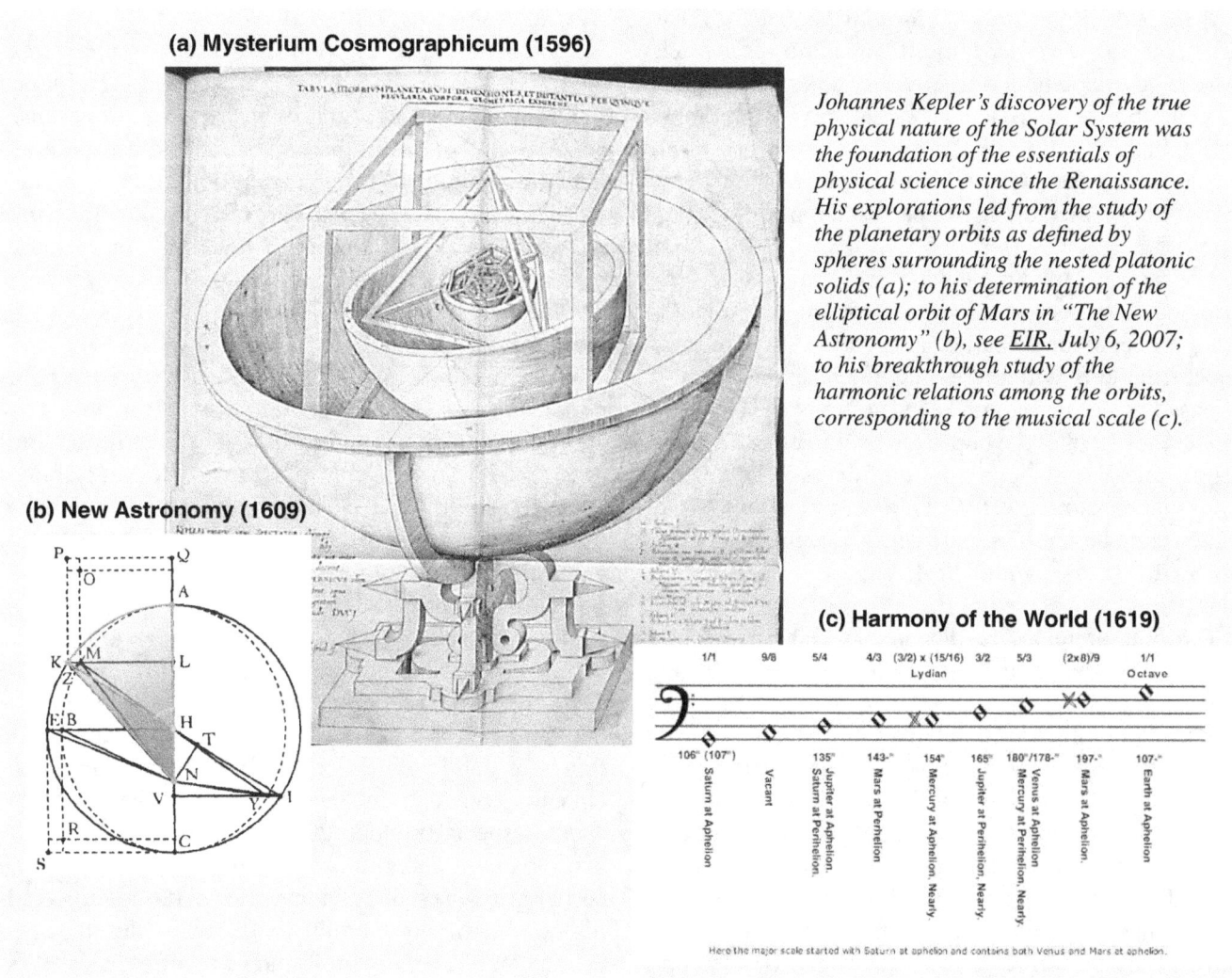

(a) Mysterium Cosmographicum (1596)

(b) New Astronomy (1609)

Johannes Kepler's discovery of the true physical nature of the Solar System was the foundation of the essentials of physical science since the Renaissance. His explorations led from the study of the planetary orbits as defined by spheres surrounding the nested platonic solids (a); to his determination of the elliptical orbit of Mars in "The New Astronomy" (b), see EIR, July 6, 2007; to his breakthrough study of the harmonic relations among the orbits, corresponding to the musical scale (c).

(c) Harmony of the World (1619)

graded to the form of mere meanings of individual words and sentences; language-culture must apprehend that which is about to become discovered as known from both the future of the speaker, and, also, his comparable forerunners before him.

My stated view, at this immediate juncture here, needs to become understood very carefully, even among the presently unwitting, as something far beyond the mere parochialisms of sense-perception as such. We must inspire the cultures of the nations with the access to the comprehension of the true meanings lodged within our Solar system (for example), meanings which are not the captive prisoners of mere sense-perceptual processes and their prejudices, but reference meanings which belong to the Solar system (as a system, independently of sense-perception *per se*).

It is precisely on this immediately fore-stated, spe-

cific account, that the otherwise seemingly lost more ancient wisdom, was often regained through the particular quality of true genius exemplified in the great fundamental scientific discoveries of the three figures from the Golden Renaissance, persons aroused by the awakening dawn of an actually modern civilization, that of the Golden Renaissance of, most emphatically, in the order (once more) of: (1) Filippo Brunelleschi, the liberator of science from mere mathematics; (2) Nicholas of Cusa, the discover of the "All;" and the discoverer of the most essential foundation of all competent physical science: (3) Johannes Kepler's, personally unique, discovery of the actuality of the Solar system.

This discovery by Kepler, which is admittedly implicit in some degrees of foresight, from the true discovery of Earth, by Eratosthenes, has been both the foundation of all essentials of known physical science today since the Renaissance. Through the means of that achievement, by Kepler himself, mankind discovered the keys to understand not only the, otherwise, previously unknowable, practical existence of the Solar system, but, by those same means, the immediate basis in foundations for mankind's escape from the virtual captivity of elementary sense-perceptual presumptions as such.[14]

The sane and the insane must not be regarded as enjoying a common standard of opinion or related, common, behavior. I shall continue to emphasize that, henceforth, here, with increasing emphasis. It is man's increased power to defend the existence of the progressive development of the human species itself,[15] which is the only tolerable standard for truthfulness in any region of this planet – and, in effect, even within regions of the Solar system beyond, as I shall emphasize that specific point in due course, within the later parts of this present report.

The commonplace predicament which causes uncertainty in popular opinion on this account, is to be recognized as the potentially fatal error of reliance on the mistakenly presumed authority of mere sense-perception itself, as such. This subject, the separation of mind, from the mere shadows of experience which we regard as sense-perception, is an indispensable separation which, in and of itself, provides the most essential precondition for a human sanity-in-fact.

So, what I have already, repeatedly identified as the triad of truly scientific genius represented by the converging elements of Brunelleschi, Cusa, and Kepler, or the later, Planck-Einstein-Vernadsky alternative, exemplify the present foundations of all competent scientific method available to our contemporaries presently: as I had done in opposition to reliance on mere sense-perception as such. Kepler's solution, as I had summarized that warning in the case in *Chapter II: The Ontology of Economy*, from my description of **"The Satan Still Operating From Inside Bertrand Russell's Corpse."**[16]

_____

14. Numerous otherwise credible modern physical scientists, including all those who remain ignorant of the essential principles of the set of discoverers, Brunelleschi, Cusa, and Kepler, remain imprisoned in encumbering incompetencies respecting the foundations of a presently efficient physical science reaching beyond the limits of the inherent ignorance of mere sense-certainties.

15. As implicitly measurable in terms of increased energy-flux density in human practice.

16. March 19, 2014, see footnote 7.

Bestiality Among Humans Now

Foremost, however, we must free our opinions from the farce which is, implicitly, any notion of the human mind as being based primarily in what is merely sense-perception. Sane, adult human beings, unless, perhaps, they are habituated drug-addicts to marijuana or other weeds of their likeness, or clinically insane otherwise, in particular, do not base their beliefs on mere sense-perceptions. Indeed, as a matter of public safety in society, the relative claims to sanity of such folk must be discounted accordingly.

Take, for example, the clinical case of recently reported suicides among secondary students in New York City schools. Include the case of the student who commits suicide under social pressures of failing grades, when the failure had been actually that of the educational system referenced, or under the burdens of the cultural conditions of the society of relevance. Who has failed, in the typical such cases?

It is the society which has failed, in most among these cases, or, more narrowly, the onset of the clinical absurdity of the secondary class imposed upon the students under the impact of the currently degenerating trends in public education (such as instruction in Euclidean geometry) during the course of the recent decades, especially since 2000 (e.g., the Bush-Cheney and Obama tenures, this far). The student has lost an earlier grip on a sense of a meaningful future life: a failing often combining brutal conditions within the society and an often more profound sense of hopeless existential defeat. Usually, the educational program itself, has homicidal effects: the sense of a meaninglessness of a life as if lived merely unto itself.

There is nothing intrinsically specific to the case of affected adolescents, or even younger children. It is present U.S. society which is the criminal in our case (in particular), especially since the close of President Bill Clinton's terms. Life under Cheney and Obama reeks of the potential for mass homicide, as in terms of deteriorating conditions of life, in terms of a deeply sensed, society-induced existential "sense of personal defeat," as also expressed in a sense of a meaninglessness of human life under such conditions, *per se*. Life, for those victims of our present society, has no longer a credible existential meaning.

This is no mere sociological phenomenon; it is the characteristic of the fanatic who sheds life readily because the continuation of human life itself has no credible meaning for him, or her: exactly what has been done

Signs of a Dark Age: suicides by high school students. "The student has lost an earlier grip on a sense of a meaningful future life: a failing often combining brutal conditions within the society and an often more profound sense of hopeless existential defeat. Usually, the educational program itself, has homicidal effects: the sense of a meaninglessness of a life as if lived merely unto itself."

to the typical American adolescent (among others) presently, and that increasingly so. The mere sight of the face of a Dick Cheney or a Barack Obama, is a drug-like effect sufficient to promote suicidal impulses of one guise, or another.

Thus, the Saudi mass-killer deployed into "9-11," and our West Coast drug addict, are victims of the same, culturally induced homicidal pathology.[17]

III. The Study of the Human Mind

The issue to be considered, here, is not that of life *per se*, but of human life.[18] The distinction of man from

beast, can not be reduced to a matter of merely relative gradations. Every human life is to be considered, in practice, as implicitly precious to all mankind, and also as essential to the continuation of progress of life on Earth in general. The ban on death-sentences can not be compromised, nor can torture of human beings be tolerated, that for the very reason of the essentially required, ontological distinction of man from beast. While we can, through animal husbandry, and, more so, through cultivation of pets, bring forth an echo-like manifestation of likeness to human behavior in pets, no animal species can ever achieve the specific quality of the viable human mind.[19]

The distinction lies within the specific domain of the human mind. It is not the body otherwise, which is sacred in the case of the human individual; it is the *noëtic* principle specific to the human mind: *the power of foreknowledge of a revolutionary change in the future of mankind.* Any adult (for example) human personal-

---

17. Since the two Chechen wars launched against Russia's Vladimir Putin, by the British Empire and its Saudi-centered connections in Africa and Asia, have been a major element in the bestiality against the United States (i.e., "9-11" under Vice-President Dick Cheney's arrangements). Veteran Nazi killers operating as a designated government in Ukraine, are a related sort of Nazi-like, or related modes of terrorist modes of epidemic bestiality polluting all continents of this planet.

18. Decent human beings are not cruel to animals, lest they, themselves, lose a grip on a sense of humanity. Let an animal to be slaughtered, not experience the terminating action. We do not wish to eat our pets, or, at the least, not to be reminded of that action. Consider the relationship to "combat fatigue" under stressed-out circumstances. But:

man is not, properly, an animal. Those persons who failed to grasp the distinction, are probably not far removed from mere beasts, if at all, on that account: the horrid perversions expressed by President Barack Obama and his purely homicidal kill-ratios, for example.

19. As a matter of principle, there is no presently competent form of generally accepted notion of the human mind as such. Specifically, the actually noëtic powers of the human mind have no exact correspondence with that of other forms of life. Man is the only species which commands access to an efficient mode of actually scientific foreknowledge of a willfully determined future. While the human brain has correspondence with the function of the human mind, the products of the discovery of truly human knowledge of universal principles generated by the human mind, are implicitly and efficiently immortal: the crucial difference of the human species, from the beasts. Unfortunately, most persons, still today, have no functional awareness of this access to this crucially distinct, superior function of the actual human mind. The cases of the discoveries by Filippo Brunelleschi, Nicholas of Cusa, Johannes Kepler, C.F. Gauss, Bernhard Riemann, Max Planck, Albert Einstein, and V.I. Vernadsky, are cases which I have emphasized in my recent series of reports. The same principle is found in Classical artistic composition, as in poetry, drama, and music, but not the common trash which passes for "popular." The accounting for this principle, is located outside the domain of merely ordinary sense-perception-as-such (e.g., crude "sense-certainty" as such).

ity who does not know a relatively efficient prescience of the actual future of history in some significant degree, is intellectually the case of a damaged mind of that human personality. This is the essentially the factor in inducing human individuals into the habits of relatively human expressions of bestiality among so-called "lower classes." Ironically, it is Wall Street's rich who tend to typify the actually most inhumanly bestial, who must not, therefore, be coddled too much, but correctly recognized as more in the category of "performing animals," than of actually human intellectual qualities of morality.

In fact, that virtually relative dehumanization of large portions of the human population, has been, typically, a legacy of the legendary, evil Zeus, and of the system of government, over those kept in slavery (especially over successive generations) generally, and of the effects of herding imposed upon those treated as inferior classes. The systematically, steep accelerating rates of downgrading of the educational systems imposed upon the majority of the United States student population generally, especially, increasingly, since the close of the 1960s, provides us a generalized measure of the moral imbecility which has taken over the trans-Atlantic cultures, most notably our own, in particular, since the closing years of the 1960s.

A Case in Point

The dependency on human sense-perception can be efficiently overcome, only through systemic insight into the relations between sense-perceptual experience and relations which reach into space (for example). Notable pre-modern discoveries in physical science, such as the measurement of the Earth, from observations of the motion of the Sun, by Eratosthenes, must be regarded as a refined case, beyond the dimensions of the known conceptions of the famous Archimedes.

The more crucial case, beyond the ancients (insofar as we presently know specifically comparable cases of measurements), had been the triadic achievement of Brunelleschi and Cusa, in the still unique achievement of Johannes Kepler in defining the Solar system *ontologically*, as only relatively rare contemporary scientists have actually understood the achievement of Kepler, still presently.

The concluding sentence of Bernhard Riemann's habilitation dissertation, is a similarly unique modern principle of physics still today. The character of those instants of science-discoveries of principle does not exist in the generality of physical-science subject-matters

presently: a travesty largely due to the bastardly pseudo-science of such number-mumblers as David Hilbert and the dupes of Bertrand Russell. The correct method for such cases is, still, the method used by Kepler for defining the Solar system, as such.

When relevant matters are carefully considered, it should not be difficult to locate the distinction of Kepler's original, actually fundamental discovery of Solar principle, from the required point of view located specifically within the presumed ontological framework common to Planck and Einstein. The definition of object has undergone a pressing requirement for a change in ontological axioms.

However, even that implication is not so simple as something which simply trying could accomplish. But, then, a greater challenge is presented, as the principle of life, particularly human life: which is quite plainly the bottom-line of the human knowledgeable experience: hence, the crucial significance of the work of V.I. Vernadsky bearing on the actual functions of the human mind.

With that, the definition of ontology itself undergoes a qualitatively higher order of ontological implications, from the object of attributed existence, to the deeper-underlying, universal principle of, immediately life, then, into the ontologically still higher human life, and, thence, the still higher notion of creativity *per se*: the water which flows, but through no same river, ever again. It is not a matter of the substance, but of the process represented.

At that stage, something conclusive has been reached here, at least: a principle, not a mere thing. Habit defies acceptance of such elemental notions. The allegedly "smallest" disappears, and the *noësis* takes control. All now has the name of creativity *per se*. The answers remain enigmas, but they are no longer, merely fantasies: push them, and see how they react, or do not react. The result? We define it as a discovered principle.

IV. The Future in the Human Mind

Heretofore, my report here, has remained, not only up to this point, but beyond, within the ordering of a conventional ticking of a clock deemed the future progress of history. In fact, the adoption, otherwise, of a more conventional view of the matter, runs directly against the most essential evidence respecting the powers, or lack of powers of the human mind. The specific distinction of the human mind, lies in the most essential fact of all true science, that all evolutionary progress of the human species is based on an achieved foreknowledge of the future. That principled fact is the most crucial, and, also, the most essential element, of the naturally predefined, elementary systemic evidence of the difference of man from beast.

It is, otherwise, unfortunately, the aspect of society in which the essentially practical matters of human progress have been, usually, neglected in an actually vicious extreme.

If you do not know the future in some significant degree, you are also, already ignorant of the meaning of the present time.

The simplest contemporary distinction to me made on that account, is appropriately illustrated by the prevalence of the outright fraud of the teaching of Euclidean geometry in schools. That has been actually a crime against humanity, not merely in part, but generally. It had been already known as a practiced crime in the text of the **Bible's Genesis** I, already since then.

The evidence to be drawn so, is elementary: no animal species can willingly discover a demonstration of the characteristic distinction of members of the human species. This fact has been well known since such cases as the systemic species-like difference in cultures separating that of Zeus (e.g., "the Greenies") and the Brometheans. Indeed, the practice of Euclidean geometry was a neo-Zeusian return to backwardness, one which had persisted in much of even modern European civilization after the achievements of Filippo Brunelleschi, Nicholas of Cusa, and Johannes Kepler, even, often, Kepler's uniquely original discovery of the principled characteristic of the Solar system, even among practicing scientists, as specifically known to me, as late as during the generation of the 1940s-1970s: that because they had been subjected to regurgitations of the archaic follies in teaching practices administered to baccalaureate scientific miseducation common in leading universities of the United States during the 1940s-1950s intervals of their baccalaureate candidacies, and beyond.[20]

For example: it is commonplace to hear, that among presumably literate graduates of secondary and higher education, that is it not possible to have foreknowledge of the future. Yet, all qualitative leaps in scientific progress, such as those of moderns such as Brunelleschi, Cusa, Kepler, Leibniz, Gauss, Riemann, Max Planck, Albert Einstein, and V.I. Vernadsky,[21] are associated with physically-principled, rather than merely pro-deductive discoveries of gains in scientific matters of universal physical (and closely related, true universal) principles, or such as Eratosthenes[22] before them.

This distinction of the human species, is shown most directly by mankind's distinguishing characteristic, the use of "fire" in all the connotations of that notion. Any adult professional who fails to recognize the essential nature of foreknowledge of the future, must be considered incompetent in the sense of being scientifically defective in relevant matters of policy-making of practice. This is commonly confessed (if only implicitly) by the person who professes himself, or herself, to be merely "practical," rather than scientifically qualified; to place the relevant emphasis, they are scientifically disqualified in rendering their choice of judgments, and, are, therefore, necessarily, suspect of being virtually Zeusians, rather than the scientifically competent Prometheans.

This disgusting lack of scientific qualification, is to be regarded as seriously in error, in light of the fact that it is the related, essential inability to distinguish man from mere beast, which is at issue practically, for society generally, on precisely this account. If you are not qualified in such knowledge, you are not qualified to define the choices for policies of practices of entire societies, but are disabled from making judgments on matters of policies respecting such more sophisticated considerations. It is not the knowledge itself, but, rather, the implications for taking such considerations into account, which defines the necessities of the principles of practice for societies: if the issue lands on your plate, you are obliged, professionally, to make yourself competent in approaching relevant solutions within the domain of that field of inquiry.[23] Indeed, the most es-

---

20. Their follies had been leftovers from an undergraduate miseducation which had taught them to ridicule the discoveries of Brunelleschi, Cusa, and Kepler's unique principle. As I had experienced this, prolifically, in both my own secondary and undergraduate university education. For example, my knowledge of the incompetence of Euclidean geometry was fully, and correctly firmly and finally, successfully established by me at the age of 14.

21. To name only the most distinguished of the absolutely most distinguished.

22. The discovery of the measure of the Earth, by Eratosthenes, gave us the earliest case of a sure-footed insight into the Solar system beyond Earth as independent of mere human sense-perception as such.

23. There are no perfectly educated people in a competently organized society, but only those who recognize that they are still being self-educated, or otherwise in respect to ever-present, matters of fresh challenges.

sential distinction of the human individual, is, that, on this account, which essentially distinguishes the heathy state of mind of man, from both the beasts and the beastly.

To clarify the issues so represented, consider the significance of our present knowledge of space, from knowledge attributed to Earthly sense-perception as such. Post the relevant argument, here, as follows.

Man & His Self-Perception

It may appear, but only mistakenly, in most approaches to the experience of sense-perception heretofore, that all of mankind's knowledge from experience, were dependent upon sense-perception. There are certain systemic features of sense-perception which are, in fact, exceptions to such a proposition; but, insofar as people depend upon sense-perception as their presumed only source of knowledge from experience, they have tended, predominantly, to overlook the systemic differences between mere sense-perception and the actually experienced, qualitative higher, cognitive functions of the human mind. Our confrontation with space, as illustrated very well by Kepler, had provided us with very strong sources of insight into the efficient experience of the higher principles lying beyond mere sense-perception as such.

Each among those considerations, when well combined, as that trio had done, in effect, provided the modern human mind with the undeniable existence of agencies superior to those of mere sense-perception. These agencies had not been unknown among what might be described as the best thinkers; but, popular features of social commerce among the masses of the population, had strongly resisted them under the influence of what might be fairly indicted as "popular common sense," and that, repeatedly, and, also often violently in social effect.[24]

Albrecht Dürer, Self-Portrait (1500). "The products of the discovery of truly human knowledge of universal principles generated by the human mind," LaRouche writes, "are implicitly and efficiently immortal: the crucial difference of the human species, from the beasts."

---

24. The cultural conflict between Christianity and the Roman Empire (and, also, the British Empire) typifies exemplary cases of respectively systemic contrasts. For example: some branches of nominal Christianity, had adopted a Zeusian (e.g., pro-feudalist) social doctrine, rather than that of such testamental authorities as the notable disciples Peter, Paul, and John. The contrary, errant interpretations, were, most commonly, adaptations to such pro-Zeusian dogmas as those of the Roman and British empires. Notable Jewish contemporaries of the early Christian authorities, such as Philo, also shared kindred social-theological outlooks for practice. The sometimes rejections of this quality of Philo's outlook among some Christians, had been, in part, a product of feudal societies' adaptations to a Zeusian legacy based in either feudalism, or the more primitive modalities. Jeanne d'Arc and the leaders of the Christian "Golden Renaissance" of such as Nicholas of Cusa, are, thus, typical of a rejection of the Zeusian moral-cultural degeneracy, and the latter degeneracy's contemporary, modern relics. Christianity, particularly in its merely nominal relics (such as the Dutch and British imperialisms launched during the 17th and 18th centuries, has been among the most grievous offenders on this account, and, thus, the typical source of the worst neo-Zeusian cult-formations. Generally, throughout contemporary society, it is the pro-Zeusian religions and their cultures, which have exerted the most depraved influence on contemporary world society generally, and the greatest degree of social-cultural backwardness, or even outright depravities. Generally, throughout contemporary society, it is relics of pro-Zeusian social-cultural backwardness still imposed upon some parts of present cultures which must be approached with science-driven progress in culture and technologies which will serve as the chief sources for remedies required.

In brief: mankind should be fairly considered as no less than an inhabitant of the Solar system (and beyond) in terms of our species' mental life and related relations. On this account, astronomy must be considered, henceforth, as the dominant feature in defining of the means and goals of human progress. This is, especially, as the power of mankind, as a species, has now grown beyond other thermonuclear-fusion standards, into the present pre- occupation with the added practical potential represented by the Solar deposits of Helium-3 accumulations available to Earth from, its Moon, as to be gathered by us as to be taken from the Moon.

Such a Helium-3 enhancement of Earth-based sources of empowerment, brings us into the prospect for such means as treatments of nearby-passing asteroids and, possibly, comets, too. These considerations foresee mankind, while otherwise still confined, essentially, to Earth for purposes of residence, has, nonetheless, the early prospect of manned (directly, or indirectly) deployment for man-directed interventions into regions into which man could not visit efficiently without extraordinary means beyond the general limits of our species' present capabilities.

Our resources, must, on first account, signify our relative freedom from narrowly-defined, Earth-bound means to be brought into the use of mankind living on Earth. Yet, insofar as we are more or less immediately within reach of nearby-space operations, the psychological distance from strict "Earth-boundness" changes the outlook of mankind-still-on-Earth, toward a Solar-based outlook, and beyond, such as the tracking of the pathway of the Solar system with respect to its passage within the Galaxy. This means a shift, emphatically in physical-scientific outlooks, to a view of life on Earth, as being one dependent on the increasing ration of a non sense-perception view of mankind's practice within the Solar system, and beyond.

This view is implicit in the achievements, this far, of the accomplishments still under way under the auspices of the missions of Max Planck, Albert Einstein, and the unique implications of the genius shown by V.I. Vernadsky.

This, the weight of consideration of merely sense-perception, must be transformed into an accelerated rate of change in mankind's outlook on the Earth-bound aspects of mere sense-perception as such. We must greet such changes, and, that, with corresponding desire for a more intimate relationship to the work of the Creator of it all.

Editorial

Since When Is Genocide Philanthropic?

In May 2009, a collection of the world's wealthiest men and women met behind closed doors at the President's House at Rockefeller University in New York City to chart out a merger of all of their combined philanthropic efforts. Seated around the elegant table were the billionaire hosts—David Rockefeller, Warren Buffett, and Bill Gates—and the invited guests, including Ted Turner, George Soros, Oprah Winfrey, Peter Peterson, Julian Robertson, Eli Broad, and then-New York Mayor Michael Bloomberg. All told, their net worth passed $130 billion.

At the initiative of Bill and Melinda Gates and Warren Buffett, the group pledged to direct all of their so-called "philanthropic activities" toward a single cause. According to news leaks from the meeting, and a subsequent series of similar meetings held around the United States, the group decided to pool their vast wealth to promote Malthusian population reduction. Media mogul Ted Turner, one of the more outspoken members of the multi-billionaires club, openly called for a 100-year period of family planning to impose a global one-child policy. At the end of the century, the world's population would be reduced to no more than 2 billion people. Not coincidentally, the same objective of mass population reduction has been the avowed commitment of the British royal family. The Royal Consort, Prince Philip, co-founder with Prince Bernhard of The Netherlands (now deceased) of the Malthusian World Wildlife Fund, has expressed his wish to be reincarnated as a deadly virus to contribute to the cause of population reduction.

As you will have read elsewhere in this issue of *EIR*, Buffett and Gates are at the center of the promotion of fracking, an oil-and-gas extraction scheme that has been a mighty cause of the depletion of the water supplies of the United States, Canada, and Mexico, west of the Mississippi River. We have now reached a point where the combination of fracking, drought, and the diversion of corn and other food for biofuels has created a food crisis that is soon to erupt as an existential crisis. For many, food-price hyperinflation will make it impossible to provide for their families. Eventually the food will simply not be there.

Is it a coincidence that Warren Buffett, the self-professed Olympian god of Omaha, who has devoted his philanthropic energies to population reduction, is behind the fracking swindle that threatens mass food shortages and starvation as early as this year?

Add to the mix the fact that another member of the mega-billionaires club, George Soros, has dedicated his "philanthropic" activities to the legalization of mind-destroying drugs—another form of genocide, which also happens to be a Federal crime. Does a picture emerge from this admittedly quick course in modern philanthropy?

Back in the 1940s, some Members of Congress raised flags over the abuse of Federal tax codes, permitting super-rich individuals to conduct subversive activities under the guise of tax-exempt charitable activity. Today's frackers and dope legalizers certainly fit the profile. Their overt commitment to radical population reduction as a "cause" befitting privileged tax relief boggles the mind.

By our standards, the promotion and execution of mass genocide is no charity. Genocide is genocide and should be called for what it is—a crime against humanity.